THE JOHN HARVARD LIBRARY

Bernard Bailyn

EDITOR-IN-CHIEF

THE JOHN HARVARD LIBRARY

LETTERS
from AMERICA

William Eddis

Edited by Aubrey C. Land

THE BELKNAP PRESS OF

HARVARD UNIVERSITY PRESS

Cambridge, Massachusetts

1969

100192

CONTENTS

v

CONTENTS

CONTENTS

CONTENTS

CONTENTS

CONTENTS

INTRODUCTION

William Eddis was a born letter-writer in a great age of letter writing. The short list alone is impressive: Bolingbroke, Horace Walpole, Lord Chesterfield. Like his more illustrious contemporaries, Eddis wrote in the grand manner, reporting news items along with his descriptions of the local scene, accounts of institutions, and sketches of important persons. All this he dressed up with the allusions and quotations that were as much a part of a proper letter in the eighteenth century as the inevitable philosophical reflections.

Of the ingredients that we have come to associate with Augustan and Georgian letters the only one missing is malice. Neither the superb innuendo of Walpole nor the sardonic bite of Chesterfield figures in the Eddis letters. Eddis moved easily in the best society in Maryland. He relished his associates, his post, his surroundings, and he wrote of them with charm and affection. His tone at times approaches the innocent and beguiling merriment of Cinderella transported miraculously to the ball. The high sin of the Mistress of the World he left to the Walpoles and Chesterfields, who would bite, and bite viciously, to hold their own in the intense society of Georgian London. But if guileless, Eddis was not naïve. His letter left for posterity the qualitative judgments of an intelligent observer of the colonial scene. Accordingly his comments are especially important for historians and general readers who would recapture the feeling of this lost world.

Readers of these attractive letters will wish that in Colonial

Maryland more than one Eddis had flourished to bring alive the contemporary scene. They may, too, wonder how he happened to produce these. His biography, sketchy when dealing with the time before he came to America, offers a clue but no firm explanation. The known events fill little more than a single paragraph.

William Eddis was born on February 6, 1738, at Northleach in the Cotswolds.[1] About the education that laid the basis for his literary style, the record stands blank. In his twenty-sixth year he married Elizabeth Mackbrand, who became the mother of his first two children, a boy and a girl. Before the birth of his daughter, Eddis had landed in London, where he took the infant for christening to St. Paul's Church, Court Garden.[2]

Though Eddis was not without patrons, his backers could not assist him to a place of profit rewarding enough to gratify his tastes. He had a passion for the theater, perhaps growing out of his boyhood friendship with William Powell, a light of the London stage. His other friends included painters and aspiring writers, among them Hannah More, who was on the threshold of her famous career. Possibly these associates guided his tastes toward writing. But if he had ambitions in letters his employment left him small time to cultivate them. For support of his family, he had the income of a petty clerk. His relief came with the appointment as Governor of Maryland of Robert Eden, brother-in-law of Frederick, Baron of Baltimore and Lord Proprietor of the Province. Eden's patronage provided a minor place for Eddis in Maryland, one that evidently served him better than his prospects in London. And so, like others with talents and tastes beyond their expectations at home, he came to America. In the autumn of 1769 he arrived in Maryland, after a

---

[1] George H. Williams, "William Eddis: What the Sources Say," *Maryland Historical Magazine*, 60 (1965), 121-131, recites the essential facts.

[2] *Ibid.*, 122.

voyage that he described as tedious, to take the post of surveyor and searcher of His Majesty's customs in the port of
Annapolis.[3]

— 2 —

The Annapolis to which Eddis came differed from port
cities to the north. Philadelphia, New York, and Boston were
all provincial capitals, but they were also commercial centers,
distributing points for the cargoes arriving almost daily in
all seasons except the depth of winter. By contrast, Annapolis
had grown into a community of official residences whose
owners formed an elite of wealth and taste. The beauty of
the Annapolis waterfront along the broad, placid Severn sur-
passed its utility. Inshore shallows discouraged ships of deep
draft, compelling them to unload on South River or sending
them to the rapidly growing port of Baltimore, thirty miles
to the north. The drifting population of sailors, the dock and
warehouse hands, and the places for their entertainment
figured in only a minor way in Annapolis. Some modest
structures along Cornhill Street, leading to State Circle,
housed artisans and their places of business. But on the
broader streets, imposing residences of the Carrolls, Taskers,
Bordleys, Dulanys, Lloyds, Chases, and Stewarts gave the
city its style and appearance.

Subconsciously, Eddis must have applied the standards of
London when he wrote home his first impressions: "This
city has more the appearance of an agreeable village, than
the metropolis of an opulent province." In population Annapolis lagged behind many provincial capitals. Fewer than
1,400 souls lived within the corporate limits, but the existence
of even that small population may be considered remarkable.
In the early days, a pair of speculators had, for a time, discouraged development of the area when they laid claim to

---

[3] Commission dated September 28, 1769, and issued by the commissioner
of the customs at Boston. His salary was £60 a year plus fees.

the whole site under color of an ancient grant that was worded rather ambiguously. Then at one time a band of brigands had threatened to raze the tiny community that had grown up in defiance of the speculators' claim, and the outlaws had actually burned the old capitol building in the dead of night. Daytime fires occurred frequently enough among the wooden houses of these early years to thin down the density of population. Ebenezer Cook probably came close to the truth in his description penned for *The Sot-Weed Factor* in 1708:

> Up to Annapolis I went,
> A City Situate on a Plain,
> Where scarce a house will keep out Rain;
> The Buildings fram'd with Cyprus rare
> Resemble much our Southwark Fair.[4]

But over succeeding decades the flimsy structures reminiscent of fair booths had given way to brick houses in Georgian style.

In fact the arrival of Eddis coincided with a burst of new building that gave the city some of the mansions which have become showplaces. Lloyd Dulany was building a massive brick house of all-header bond on Conduit Street at a cost in construction alone of £10,000. Across town on the corner of King George and Northeast Streets, Samuel Chase had begun a three-story mansion which shortly exceeded his pocketbook. He sold the unfinished structure for £3,000 to Colonel Edward Lloyd, who was prepared to lay out the estimated £6,000 needed to complete the design, including, among other appointments, mahogany doors with silver hinges and latches. For wealthy patrons the architectural services of an expert, William Buckland, were available.

[4] Ebenezer Cook, "The Sot-Weed Factor; or a Voyage to Maryland. A Satyr" (London, 1708), in Bernard C. Steiner, *Early Maryland Poetry* (Fund Publication No. 36, Maryland Historical Society, Baltimore, 1900), pp. 19-20.

Somehow Eddis sensed the atmosphere of enterprise in Annapolis, for he modified his observation on its rural appearance with the claim that Annapolis would be within a few years one of the best-built cities in America. "A spirit of improvement," he added, "is predominant."

— 3 —

Eddis found Annapolis society much more to his taste than the external appearance of the city. Almost as soon as he had lost his sea legs he joined the social whirl. In mid-October he accompanied Governor Eden and his lady on a progress to the Eastern Shore for his first taste of the hospitality in the great country houses. By December he had made the exclusive party that kept Christmas at Colonel Fitzhugh's country seat, Rousby Hall, in Calvert County. Untrammeled by family responsibilities before the arrival of his wife and son, Eddis moved easily into the circle about the governor — the first families. The humble customs clerk who had seen the glitter of London's *haut monde* as a bystander on the fringes now experienced the coquetry and small talk at the very center. His letters underwent a subtle transformation; the note of condescension vanished. The quasi-bachelor saw provincial women in the seductive glow of candlelight and found them "fashionable and handsome." Parties were frequent and gay. Hosts spared no pains to insure the pleasure of their guests. Dancing, cards, decor, collations — all passed scrutiny of the observant newcomer.

Instinctively Eddis had responded to some basic modality in capital life. Annapolis society knew good manners and insisted on decorum. Yet it had a touch of the delirium of a *nouveau riche* community and some of its rawness. Like San Francisco in 1900 or Dallas of post-World War II, the tiny capital on the Severn focussed on itself the power and riches of a country being laid under tribute to man. The untapped resources of nature and the animal energy of toilers turning them to service were reflected in a kind of oasis culture in the city. Beyond lay the wilderness. Within, society ordered its round of pleasures with a kind of robust vigor that sometimes overstepped the limits of gusto. Frontier manners occasionally intruded in the highest places, as when the convivial merchant, Robert De Butts, took to "rastling at the Governor's . . . drunken frolic [and] so much alarmed [Mrs. Eden] . . . at the disturbance they made in the house that she miscarried." [5] The violent tenor of life extended beyond the lower orders.

— 4 —

Eddis reported Annapolis and its society admirably as well as, in some measure, the province at large. But of the broader context he gives occasional glimpses only. He focussed on the near-at-hand — the social round and capital politics. These formed the subjects of daily conversation among his knot of intimates and the larger circle of his associates. With the crude and commonplace — farmers and laborers — his contacts were few and his interest was even less. England had her poor, the masses in city and countryside; they were no novelty to Eddis, either back home or in Maryland. Neither were they new to Dr. Alexander Hamilton, who like Eddis had moved in the best circles, or any of the other visitors who have left accounts of Colonial Maryland. And yet these ordinary people figured in the Chesapeake scheme of things far more importantly than the "meaner sort" back home in British affairs.

For one thing, the humble folk had the numbers that counted in a rather different way in Maryland. A cross-section of planting families in Eddis' day shows approximately one family in twenty with sufficient wealth to put it in the class of "great planters," the squirearchy whose coun-

[5] Charles Carroll of Carrollton to Charles Carroll, August 9, 1771, *Maryland Historical Magazine*, 32 (1937), 200-201.

try places caught the fancy of Eddis: Colonel Fitzhugh of Rousby Hall, for instance. The other nineteen families showed a wide range of sumptuary conditions from near wealthy to bleak poverty. A recent statistical analysis of estates below the great-planter level divides them into three groups of descending affluence. Planters with estates in personalty between £500 and £1,000, nearly 10 per cent, had an obviously good life: bonded labor, good houses, furniture, and many of the luxuries. Those whose estates ranged from £100 to £500, about 30 per cent, if not blessed with the adornments, still had ample livings. The largest number of planting families, nearly 60 per cent, had estates of £100 or less and lived on the economic margin. At first glance these proportions do not appear markedly different from the economic stratification of England in the same decades. If anything, the lowest economic stratum in England comprised an even larger percentage of families, because it included not only the urban workmen but also the numerous folk of the countryside — the cotters, shepherds, and the like — who fall under the heading, "rural proletariat." Excepting a handful of artisans and mechanics in Annapolis, these two propertyless elements, urban and rural, did not exist in Colonial Maryland. Poor or affluent, Marylanders were planters, even those who leased their land. Nevertheless, the social order of the Chesapeake ran to variety rather than to uniformity in the sumptuary conditions of life. The great planters of textbook fame comprised a small fraction of the total. They built the gracious homes, exhibited the family portraits, gave lavish entertainments, and left behind in the family archives the letters, diaries, and memoirs from which a picture of the "planting order" can be reconstructed. Those in the ranks below have become the invisible people of the Chesapeake.[6]

[6] Cf. Aubrey C. Land, "Economic Base and Social Structure: The Northern Chesapeake in the Eighteenth Century," *Journal of Economic History*, 25 (1965), 639-654.

It is essential to bring these small planters up to the level of visibility and to understand their role. For from their ranks rose the great planters, as shoots from a fertile seed bed. The emergence of these first fortunes in Colonial Maryland is a surprising and fascinating spectacle. The ascent from straitened circumstances to affluence sometimes took place within the lifespan of a single person, the architect of the family fortune. Such a man, even though in the top bracket of wealth, could not forget his humble origin nor entirely forsake its ways.

There can be no doubt about the style of life among the poorest and largest element of Maryland planters — those with estates of £100 or less. Thousands upon thousands of inventories listing every scrap of personal property speak of the poverty of their material circumstances. As planters — and they too were planters — they produced small crops, somewhere between 800 and 2500 pounds of tobacco. These cash crops brought them annual incomes that ranged from £3 to £15 a year, enough for such bare necessities as hoes, thread, and oznaburg, which they purchased from the local merchant. For the rest of their living they looked to their kitchen gardens, corn crops, and livestock. Their swine shuffled for themselves in nearby woodlands, feeding on acorns and roots, breeding promiscuously until owners cropped their ears to prove possession. Their cattle similarly fended for themselves, providing meat in winter and milk the year 'round. Hunting, though a diversion from the tedium of work, was less than a sport. Small planters were pothunters and their quarry relieved the monotony of salt or pickled meat in winter.

Eddis would doubtless have shared the feeling of Dr. Alexander Hamilton, whose fastidious tastes revolted at the sight of countrymen sitting down to their repast. On his travels Hamilton encountered a couple who invited him to share "a homely dish of fish without any kind of sauce," which was their dinner.

They desired me to eat, but I told them I had no stomach. They had no cloth upon the table, and their mess was in a dirty, deep, wooden dish which they evacuated with their hands, cramming down skins, scales, and all. They used neither knife, fork, spoon, plate, or napkin because, I suppose, they had none to use. I looked upon this as a picture of the primitive simplicity practiced by our forefathers long before the mechanic arts had supplied them with instruments for the luxury and elegance of life.[7]

Doubtless Hamilton guessed right about knives, table-cloths, and napkins. Such luxuries show up rarely in the inventories of their personal estates. It is most likely, too, that table manners of all small planters lacked something in elegance. Their whole style of life would have appeared coarse to Hamilton or to Eddis. Their pastimes included such sports as gander-pulling, cudgelling, and eye-gouging. They had strong tastes that could stomach violence and bloodshed. Most countrymen in Maryland would have found the bear pits of Elizabethan days exactly the right tonic for a dull afternoon. All this came naturally. They traced their descent from a boisterous ancestry and this tradition had by no means died out in England. But the churl in England, fresh from the bear pits, would not have presumed to invite a gentleman to share his meal, nor would he have ignored the marks of respect due the better sort. Eddis and Hamilton could no more accept the egalitarian implications of lower-class conduct than they could approve the personal code and the manners of these people, so clearly their inferiors. Yet, precisely those qualities that offended Hamilton had carried these planters through the pioneering that had

[7] Carl Bridenbaugh, ed., *Gentleman's Progress: The Itinerarium of Dr. Alexander Hamilton, 1744* (Chapel Hill, 1948), p. 8.

tamed the raw wilderness not many years before, actually within the memory of living men.

And it was with some of the same crudeness and gusto that a few planters from the lower strata drove along the road to fortune. Obviously returns of a few pounds sterling from tobacco crops hardly covered the barest necessities, much less provided a surplus. But in a growing country other opportunities opened to the enterprising and imaginative. The Maryland economy rested on a solid agricultural base and the labor force devoted its energies to cultivating the field crop. But that field crop was a cash crop; agriculture was not subsistance but commercial. The significant rewards that led to fortune lay in services that were vital to a commercial agriculture and accrued to men who had the wit to operate credit and marketing mechanisms. A planter who could supply a few neighbors with goods and take their tobacco in return became a petty merchant. If he had a plantation of even modest size, he might become a landlord, leasing unused land to destitute newcomers or to indentured servants after they gained their freedom. In these small ways the enterprising moved a step ahead economically of their fellows who were content to till their tobacco fields and raise their food crops. For the planter with zeal and insight these simple beginnings were first steps. The full scope of opportunity included merchandising, land speculation, money-lending, manufacturing, and one important professional calling — the practice of law. It was in the role of entrepreneur in these lucrative callings rather than by planting pure and simple that men built the fortunes which distinguished them from the common run.

Case studies of the great planting families are a good antidote to the moonlight-and-magnolias view of the "planter." In the first years of the century several of the first families rose from modest circumstances to wealth and prominence. Details differ but the pattern of advance held true for both branches of Carrolls, the Catholic and the Protestant lines, for the Bordleys, the Dulanys, and the Macnemaras. Daniel Dulany the elder came to Maryland in the late summer of 1703 as an indentured servant and served his term as a law clerk to an attorney in the southern counties. Thereafter he became successively a distinguished lawyer, a landlord, merchant, iron manufacturer, and land speculator. Three marriages into established planting families brought him social éclat. Furthermore he held three lucrative offices in the proprietary establishment. Almost fifty years to a day after he arrived he died in the fullness of wealth and honor, leaving behind three sons already lavishly endowed, three daughters married with handsome dowries into wealthy planting families, and an immense estate in land, slaves, commercial assets, and personal property.

The emergence of this merchant-planter elite was of immense importance both economically and politically. Their enterprise kept the Maryland economy from stagnating altogether or from coming by default under outside control. They furnished services vital to commercial agriculture. As merchants they financed the small planters; as land speculators they distributed acreage to the land hungry; as monied men they made loans to tradesmen and artisans. In short, these functions brought them into the main stream of commercial capitalism. As capitalists some profited handsomely; others fell by the wayside as bankrupts. The planting society had its own way of rewarding the economically successful, by preferring the able to social leadership and by elevating them to political office.

The resemblances between Chesapeake planter-merchants and their northern commercial brethren, with whom the Calvinist outlook is usually associated, go beyond the crude connection of worldly success with divine favor. The behavior of both exemplifies the doctrine of work. Too often the planter is made the improvident, who turned to British merchant houses for ever more loans to support his mindless extravagance. Some did just that; the records are clear on the facts. But the records are also unambiguous in speaking of many more planters who had not fallen into the toils of indebtedness and who actually had sterling balances with British merchants or sterling assets in England. Few of them had holdings even approaching in magnitude those of Colonel Benjamin Tasker, who died the summer before William Eddis arrived in Maryland. Tasker left to each of his four daughters £2,500 sterling and to his four eldest grandsons £1,000 sterling each. Putting Tasker aside as an extraordinary case, the student of the northern Chesapeake finds enough instances of sterling balances among affluent merchant-planters to suggest that the debt question in its classic formulation needs refining if not complete revision. It would be rash to follow Thomas Jefferson's dictum that planters handed down debts from father to son until they became "a species of property attached to certain great British merchant houses"; something like the opposite may be closer to the truth.

Nowhere did the consequences of economic success appear more conspicuously than in provincial politics. The great planters filled public offices with such regularity that scholars have spoken of their political dominion as the rule of a planter oligarchy. Election did not, however, come automatically to sons of the "long-tailed families." Across the Potomac in Virginia, where conditions closely resembled those of Maryland, Landon Carter failed at the polls because he refused to "familiarize" with the electorate. Small producers had the numbers and their suffrages determined elections. Eddis noted that "an idea of equality also seems generally to prevail and the inferior order of people pay but little external respect to those who occupy superior stations." George Washington, a distant neighbor of Carter, accepted the realities and took to "swilling the planters with bumbo."

In Maryland, too, punchbowl and cider keg figured promi-nently in the election proceedings of well-to-do candidates. But to attribute political victory to plying the electorate with liquor would be a serious misreading. The treat merely sym-bolized the concord between community and candidate de-manded by the voters. The qualities the electorate sought in their representative were those which made for success in the world of affairs and most often the choice fell on the individual who had manifested these unmistakably in that combination of planting and commerce so characteristic of Chesapeake fortunes. The voters of Anne Arundel county, in which Annapolis lay, sent Dr. Charles Carroll, a wealthy merchant, for fifteen years as their delegate to the assembly; and after his death they sent his son, Charles Carroll, Bar-rister, to the same post.

The ultimate test of solidarity between top wealth and the lower economic strata was the faith these representatives kept with their poorer constituents. Decade after decade the House of Delegates declined to vote funds for worthy causes — a governor's house, public education, a lighthouse — to avoid levying insupportable taxes on low income producers. Anyone who wonders why investment in the public sector lagged can find at least part of the answer in the refusal of elected representatives, nearly all of them well-off, to over-burden their many constituents who lived on the margin. The wealthy knew intimately the economic circumstances of small planters not only because they had grown out of their ranks but also because their portfolios bulged with the obligations of these small fry: the mortgages, notes of hand, and book debts. About this local indebtedness we know, and in overwhelming detail. The great planters held it and held it exclusively, except in areas where British and Scottish fac-torage had intruded. And yet these same small planters, debt-ridden almost to a man, preferred their successful neighbors to office as often as election day came around. Behind this mentality lay convictions rooted in common origins and common purposes. The great planters preserved this harmony. They never became a parasitic class and few of them lost the common touch.

Eddis did not entirely miss the elemental power of American society and he occasionally remarks on past progress and potentialities for future growth: "This colony is making a rapid progress to wealth, power, and population." But his feeling for its mystique remained that of a cultivated European, different in kind from the instinctive adjustment the country-born had made. He found "the idea of equality" worth noting and seemed a little put off by the absence of deference among the lower orders to those who had "superior stations." His own predilections and interests lay with the superior element. He delighted in their company, their clubs, and their sports. Annapolis had entered a brilliant epoch, a kind of golden age. Doubtless Eddis had not expected quite the social sophistication he found, but threw himself into the revels with zest.

Social clubs in Annapolis had roots, not very deep in time to be sure, but nonetheless sturdy. In 1745 "Sandy" Hamilton and a few boon companions had formed the Tuesday Club, dedicated to fun and frolic. Its successor, the Homony Club, carried on the tradition with opulence befitting the wealth and position of its membership: Governor Eden, Daniel Dulany the younger, Jonathan Boucher, Thomas Johnson, and kindred spirits. Eddis joined this select company, by election, in 1771, and entered enthusiastically into the mock-legal proceedings.

> I'm told Billy Eddis, may he never miscarry,
> Is canvassing votes to be next Secretary,

wrote Jonathan Boucher about a month after the admission of Eddis, adding

And as he's a man of profound erudition,
Discovered but lately e'en since his admission
There's no room to doubt without making such pothers
He'll acquit himself in it much better than others.[8]

Eddis went on to become Poet Laureate, Secretary of Foreign Affairs, and eventually President. With the more sedate clubs, the St. George Society, Masonic Club, and the St. Andrews Society, he had little to do. The aura of magnificence around Homony doings appears in an advertisement in the *Maryland Gazette* on November 25, 1773, offering a reward for missing club minutes, a folio volume bound in green vellum: one hundred guineas cash with "no questions asked."

No doubt Annapolis theatricals colored Eddis' impression of the capital scene. His was the eye of the devotee and the critic, the lifetime friend of William Powell, star of the London stage. He found a community of devotion among his Maryland cronies, who had enjoyed successive seasons since 1752, when the Murray-Kean company played typical contemporary fare in Annapolis: *The Busy Body, Beau Stratagem, A Bold Stroke for a Wife.* Then in 1760 the Hallam company began annual visits with a similar repertoire. Obviously pleased by the opening of a new theater in 1771, Eddis wrote that performances came fully up to the level of the English provincial theater, with no intention of bestowing a dubious compliment.

The Annapolis races had long before his time become a fixture of the social season and won favorable comment from him. Governor Samuel Ogle had set the fashion of importing blooded horses during his second term of office, 1747-1751, and the Taskers, his wife's family, avidly followed his lead. The younger set of horse fanciers organized an exclusive

[8] Records of the Homony Club, Instituted December 22, 1770, folio 68. MS., Historical Society of Pennsylvania.

Jockey Club, which took the racing season in hand and made it a social occasion for the Chesapeake tidewater, complete with balls, dinners, and performances at the theater.[9] In 1771 the Annapolis races attracted the elite of Chesapeake horseflesh, including Alexander Spotwood's Apollo and Colonel Edward Lloyd's imported mare, Nancy Bywell. Yet a visitor from Mount Vernon made eight successive entries in his diary for the days he attended without mentioning one horse or single match, not even the Jockey Club race for a purse of one hundred guineas. Instead Major Washington set down a record of his attendance at plays, balls, and coffee house soirées.[10]

Understandably, Eddis did not comment in detail on tradesmen and artisans of Annapolis, the humbler citizens whose services made gracious living possible for the affluent. Neither did William Black, or Lord Adam Gordon, nor a host of other visitors who stopped in Maryland. Eddis could not have missed notices of persons in the trades appearing weekly in the *Maryland Gazette,* published by Anna Catharine Green and her sons after the death of Jonas Green in 1767. William Faris, watchmaker and silversmith, offered wares "equal to those of London." The bookseller and stationer, William Aikman, advertized the classics as well as the latest political pamphlets.[11] A cut lower, the tailors, hatters, and seamstresses furnished another kind of service. Their collective efforts contributed to the charm of Annapolis living, to the air that clings to a town of official residences. Eddis thought the quick adoption of English fashions in Annapolis astonishing and professed to find "very little difference . . . in the manners of the wealthy colonist and

[9] Eddis was a member of the Jockey Club.

[10] John C. Fitzpatrick, ed., *The Diaries of George Washington* (Boston, 1925), II, 34-35.

[11] Aikman did not disdain orders for imported beer, wine, and Cheshire cheese which he sold as a sideline. *Maryland Gazette,* November 10, 1774.

the wealthy Briton," except perhaps, though he did not mention the fact, that wealthy colonists adopted him and made him one of their set.

— 6 —

His first four years in Maryland were the most pleasant for Eddis. Soon after his arrival, repeal of the Townshend Acts relaxed the tensions he had initially noticed. He observed that party attachments did not seem to interfere with social intercourse. Once the strain of the Townshend taxes was eased, the political boil slowed to a simmer. A Maryland contemporary, Charles Carroll of Carrollton, ruefully declared that issues had evaporated altogether. "This is a dead time with us. Politics are scarce talked of." In this interlude of quiet Eddis prospered. His wife and son joined him in the early summer of 1770. By September 1772 he had fulfilled the three-year residence requirement for appointment to office in the provincial establishment. On the twenty-second of the month the governor appointed him commissioner of the paper currency office — the "loan office" referred to in these letters — at an annual salary of £90, with perhaps another £10 in fees. Eddis held this post concurrently with his surveyorship, worth £60 a year. He added further to his income by accepting appointment as deputy to the Lord Proprietor's agent and receiver general, Daniel of St. Thomas Jenifer, who paid him £60 a year. Altogether these combined salaries had put him beyond the straitened days he had known back home where he had been among those "disgusted with the frowns of fortune in their native land." If not wealthy, he had acquired a sufficient stake to qualify for appointment as justice of the peace in Anne Arundel county. The modest per diem allowances of county court justices brought Eddis little income, but the prestige attaching to this post of trust and responsibility made a real difference in his community standing. He might well have begun to think of himself as a Marylander.

Then suddenly at the end of 1773 his world began falling apart. "A spirit of discontent universally prevails," Eddis wrote home in November. Thereafter disasters followed in rapid order: the Boston Tea Party, the Intolerable Acts, the Peggy Stewart affair. Long before the cycle had run its course he was writing, "All America is in a flame."

After 1774 the Eddis letters report the coming of the revolution. The author was at once a spectator and a minor participant, putting out his oar, not very effectively it proved, to stave off the ultimate disaster that lay ahead, as yet unclear and undefined, but for that reason ominous and sinister.

From the beginning of the troubles Eddis left no doubt in the minds of his correspondents about the feelings of Americans toward the new look in imperial arrangements and, specifically, toward taxation. "The colonists are unanimous," he repeated with variations. Maryland, he thought, stood at the top of the moderate list. Even after the established provincial government had proved unable to cope with the crisis and an extra-legal convention had moved into the vacuum, Eddis described the proceedings as "regular and moderate." At times he almost seemed to agree with the ideological position of the colonials themselves, though he confessed he could not pretend to the kind of competence in constitutional theory that would permit him to take a dogmatic stand.

During the swift-moving days of 1775 Eddis was acutely aware that colonies and mother country were running on collision courses. To help avert the crash, the appeal to arms, he turned to the newspaper. Under the pseudonym, "A Friend to Amity," he admits that the real problem is determining the means of redress for American grievances. The colonists must not expose themselves to the same charge they were making against parliament by levying arbitrarily on citizens for arms. Let "reason and moderation hold the scale in every important determination," he recommended.

Torn himself, but clear that the appeal to arms would not answer, Eddis developed a kind of conspiratorial theory to account for American "frenzy." He saw about Maryland a few "busy, turbulent spirits" who, from motives of ambition, avarice, or discontent, agitated the passions of the multitude. Beside the danger of a break with the mother country Eddis saw his essential conception of government threatened by Tom, Dick, and Harry, upstarts inspired by ranting demagogues. By mid-summer the worst had happened. On July 25, 1775, he wrote home, "government is now almost totally annihilated, and power transferred to the multitude." The same specter haunted the dreams of his few associates who later became Tories.

Already Eddis had foreseen the possibility that he would have to leave Maryland. He took the precaution of sending his wife and young son back to England but put off final decision for almost a year, until June of 1776 when independence was clearly imminent. Only then did he ask for an exit pass and for some time to wind up the business of the paper currency office. On March 27, 1777, he put a notice in the *Gazette*:

> I intend to leave Maryland in a short time.
> William Eddis

On June 7 he boarded ship and, after many delays along the route, landed two days after Christmas at Ilfracombe in Cornwall.

Eddis completed his American tour a few weeks before his fortieth birthday. The truly memorable years of his life were behind him and he must often have looked back on them as a kind of idyllic interlude. Actually he lived another forty-eight years, to the age of eighty-eight. But they were mainly colorless years, many of them filled with the sort of frustrations he had known before going out to Maryland and a few of them marred by personal grief. In 1778 Eddis received an annual allowance of £100 sterling to compensate for the salaries he had lost when he left the colonies. On this paltry income he existed for the next decade. A few months after his return home his wife died. In 1784 he was married a second time, to Mary Upton, who in due course presented him with four children; the eldest, a boy, he named Eden for his sometime benefactor.[12]

When a Royal Commission undertook to settle claims of persons who had suffered because of their loyalty to the crown, Eddis presented a memorial that affords a glimpse at the quality of his life: "your memorialist has remained several years in a most disagreeable state of indolence and uncertainty subjected to many heavy and unavoidable expenses without the shadow of any provision excepting the allowance which he has hitherto received." Toward the end of January 1787 he appeared in person before the commissioners to give testimony on his memorial. The final decision gave him £180 a year for life.

If Eddis suffered somewhat in self-esteem while he lived bereft of emoluments and dignities he had once enjoyed, he had his moment of pride in 1792. Back in Maryland he had occasionally had the gratification of seeing bits of his prose and verse printed in the *Gazette*. Now a decade and a half afterwards he experienced the pleasures of authorship in a new way when C. Dilly published the *Letters from America* with a list of 824 subscribers.

After this point the record of his life thins to almost nothing. He lived on with his memories and a modest income until his death on December 14, 1825, a few weeks before his eighty-eighth birthday.

[12] Williams gives the known information, mostly from the Loyalist Transcripts, on pp. 129-131 of "William Eddis."

The *Letters from America* have been extensively quoted by historians. Like general readers, professionals are captivated by the freshness and charm of Eddis' writing. His letters read well whether he is describing Annapolis society, indentured servitude, or a trip to the west country. He wrote clearly even when his sentences ran beyond the length of editorial toleration. If he had a secret, it was the literary formula of the best letter writers of his day: the gentleman wrote to please.

Of course he informed also. Matter was an ingredient as well as manner. Eddis had an observant eye. His letter describing the proprietary land system is a good introduction to this thorny subject. His letter on servitude could similarly serve as a source reading for students unacquainted with the varieties of indentures and the conditions of service. Eddis did not hesitate to interpret or to pass judgment. He let his correspondents know that he took a dim view of indentured servitude. The victims, he said, "groan beneath a worse than Egyptian bondage." But his interpretation can be distinguished from his facts, which were accurate when he reported the evidence of his own eyes.

Beside the felicitous combination of matter and manner Eddis had another strength. He could tell a good story. His narrative of adventures during his exit from the Chesapeake, when he played touch-and-go with provincial officials, boatmen, and the British navy, builds up genuine suspense.

A decade and a half after Eddis wrote the last of these letters collected here he, or to follow his conceit, some of his friends, had the happy idea of publishing them. The instinct was right. Not only have students made good use of these letters, mining the facts, quoting phrases, and citing analyses, general readers have found they stand well as a whole and provide an account by a sympathetic observer of an important sector of American history during a critical period. As Eddis talks intimately to his friends, he takes us back to a world he saw vanishing.

Aubrey C. Land

A NOTE ON THE TEXT

The *Letters from America* as printed in 1792 cannot be considered archaic in the same sense that an Elizabethan text would be. Yet some of the older printing practices persisted, enough indeed to require alterations to bring the Eddis text into conformity with modern style. The following notes state and explain the rules that have guided preparation of this edition.

Mistakes noted on the errata page of the printer are silently incorporated in this edition and the old errata sheet disappears.

Antique faces and abbreviations are replaced by forms now in use. The long "s" changes to the familiar form and the ubiquitous "&c" becomes "etc." Such abbreviations as "Dec." are expanded.

In spelling, three rules are observed. (1) Modern spelling replaces older forms, as for example "tithe" for "tythe" and "Chesapeake" for "Chesapeak." (2) Misspellings of proper names are silently corrected: "Sharpe" for "Sharp." (3) Where Eddis follows a contemporary practice of using an initial followed by a dash for a proper name the editor has supplied the missing letters in brackets (if the person can be identified) when this form appears for the first time. Thereafter the name is substituted without further apparatus. For example "Mr. C——" becomes "Mr. C[hamier]," and thereafter simply "Mr. Chamier."

Like most eighteenth-century writers Eddis (or his compositor) sowed capital letters liberally through the text. For common nouns, such as assembly and tobacco, the capitals become small letters in this edition. Similarly, governor, colonel, and the like are put in lower case except when prefixed to a proper name.

In punctuation Eddis sinned on the side of overstopping. Like many of his contemporaries, he used stops to guide the voice in reading aloud, while today our practice seeks to guide the mind in seeing through the grammatical construction. He particularly overworked the comma. These have been silently removed (a) when they appear between a subject and a verb without intervening appositive matter, and (b) when they replace a tacit relative. Colons occasionally become semicolons to preserve the symmetry of a series. A few semicolons become commas for the same reason. Superfluous quotation marks are dropped. Although the long sentences invite division, the editor has, except in three places, resisted breaking them up. With these exceptions punctuation changes have been made within the original sentence structure.

Finally it should be noted that the list of 824 subscribers is omitted in this edition.

The original footnotes — indicated by symbols (*, †, etc.) — have been retained and occasional footnotes by the editor — indicated by superior numerals — have been added.

A.C.L.

LETTERS

FROM

AMERICA

HISTORICAL AND DESCRIPTIVE

COMPRISING

OCCURRENCES

FROM 1769 TO *1777* INCLUSIVE

BY

William Eddis

INTRODUCTION

If an apology for the publication of these letters be thought as necessary by the readers as it is by the author, he has only to say, and however hackneyed such excuse may be considered, he can say it with great truth, that his appearance in print is more owing to the suggestion of some partial friends than to his own intentions.

The author arrived on the American continent in the year 1769, and settled at Annapolis under the patronage and protection of the then governor of Maryland: from his situation there, he became intimately acquainted with the leading characters of every party in that province, and with every event which occurred subsequent to his own arrival, until the unfortunate misunderstanding which arose between the parent state and the colonies rendered it impossible for everyone like him, sincerely and steadily attached to the former, to continue in the country.

What he saw and observed from the first period of his residence there he occasionally communicated to his friends in England; and as he had the opportunity of seeing and observing much, it has been conceived by some respectable characters, for whose judgment he has the greatest deference, that the correspondence originally intended for private amusement only contained matter sufficiently interesting to engage the attention of the public.

The former part of these letters will be found to give a description of the country, government, trade, manners, and customs of the inhabitants; the latter, the rise and

3

gradual progress of the civil dissension, which is not perhaps so well known, at least so far as the province of Maryland was concerned, as are the consequences which attended it.

The conclusion will not, it is hoped, be thought the least interesting part of the work, as it represents the difficulties and dangers to which the author was exposed from his loyalty and unshaken attachment to the British constitution.

LETTERS

WRITTEN FROM

AMERICA

LETTER I

Yorktown, Virginia, August 30, 1769

I am, my dear friend, at length safely landed on the American continent. Our voyage has been tedious; we have encountered hard gales, and contrary winds; but of these I think no more. I am now become an inhabitant of a new world; and I enter into it not only with the common feelings of a stranger, whose attention is engaged by the novelty of every surrounding object, but with the more interesting reflection that this country is not more new to me than are my hopes and expectations in it; and that I am here under the patronage of new friends to engage in new pursuits. With this impression I cannot but form an ideal connection between what I see and what I feel. I mean not, however, that this should at all influence the narrative which I shall occasionally transmit to you; *that,* as far as is in my power, shall contain no more than what may be supposed naturally to suggest itself to any indifferent spectator whom curiosity or amusement has carried into a distant country.

I will begin with acquainting you that the situation of this town is exquisitely beautiful, and the adjacent country very romantic and picturesque. The noble Chesapeake is full in view, which, in the narrowest part, is at least ten miles broad, and runs a course of near three hundred, navigable for the largest ships. Many considerable rivers discharge themselves into this bay, by which the advantages of commerce are extended to the interior country; and planters whose habitations are far remote from the ocean receive at their own doors by water conveyance the various productions of distant nations.

From hence to Annapolis, the destined scene of my future pursuits, is two hundred miles; for which place I shall embark on board a schooner the instant I receive my baggage, and hope speedily to impart the particulars of a most favorable reception.

Chesapeake Bay, September 1st

Yesterday I made an excursion to Williamsburg, the metropolis of Virginia, the situation of which is by no means equal to Yorktown. The capital where the delegates of the people assemble is neat and elegant; the college and the governor's palace are likewise handsome edifices; but I did not distinguish any other buildings which particularly merited observation. I was, however, greatly entertained by the variegated beautiful prospects, lofty woods, and highly cultivated plantations which presented themselves to me in every direction.

I am now on my passage for Annapolis; a gentle breeze wafts us pleasantly on our course; the day is splendid and the interesting and magnificent objects which continually strike the eye infinitely exceed the utmost powers of description. Innumerable vessels of different denominations are floating in every point of view, which add to the grandeur of the scene and impress the mind with agreeable ideas of commercial advantages.

The course we are steering is nearly south;[1] we have passed many noble rivers on both sides the bay, particularly the Potomac, on the western shore, which at the entrance is several miles in breadth and is navigable for ships of great burden to Alexandria, about forty leagues from its influx. At a small distance above that place are some considerable falls, which interrupt the navigation of vessels further up the country; but I am informed that a plan is in agitation to remove this obstruction; and should success attend the execution, it is scarcely conceivable to what an immense distance commerce may be then extended.

The Potomac separates Virginia from Maryland; but there are counties belonging to each province on both sides the bay. In the Maryland government, the division is nearly equal; but in that of Virginia, their territory on the western shore is infinitely more extensive, more populous, and more important than on the eastern.[2]

These immense waters are diversified with an infinite number of islands of the most varied and beautiful appearance. Some are cultivated; others entirely covered with lofty, valuable timber. It is almost impossible, on viewing the natural advantages of this country, to avoid anticipating the future political and commercial importance of America.

A few weeks since, the Thames was the most considerable river I had ever beheld; it is now, comparatively, reduced to a diminutive stream: but may its real importance

[1] Read "north."

[2] Only two Virginia counties, Accomac and Northampton, lie on the eastern shore. In Eddis' time the seven Maryland counties on the eastern shore almost exactly matched those of the western shore in population, wealth, and political weight.

7

increase to the end of time! May the wealth of all nations flow in with every tide, to the encouragement of arts and manufactures and to the general advancement of the riches and prosperity of Britain!

Early tomorrow, I hope to land at Annapolis. The cliffs which bound the entrance of the Severn are now in view; but the wind is too light and the distance too remote to permit us to entertain a hope of reaching the harbor before morning.

Annapolis, September 4th

Early yesterday I was safely landed at my desired port. The master of the schooner conducted me to a tavern where, after a slight repast, I made the necessary preparations to appear before the governor.

My reception was equal to my warmest wishes. The deportment of Governor Eden[3] was open and friendly. He invited me to meet a party at dinner, and I took leave till the appointed hour with a heart replete with joy and gratitude.

Understanding that I was in time for divine service, I availed myself of an immediate opportunity to offer up my fervent acknowledgements at the throne of grace, and to entreat Heaven to dispense blessings on those with whom my fate is inseparably connected.

The exterior appearance of the church has little to recommend it, but the congregation was numerous. The solemn offices were performed with a becoming devotion, and my mind was perfectly in unison with the important duties of the day.

On my return to the governor he introduced me in the most obliging terms to several persons of the highest re-

[3] Sir Robert Eden (1741-1784), governor of Maryland, 1769-1776. Eden was married to Caroline Calvert, sister of Frederick, Lord Baltimore, Proprietor of Maryland.

spectability in the province. He treated me with the utmost kindness and cordiality, assured me of his strongest disposition to advance my future prosperity, and gave me an unlimited invitation to his hospitable table.

I could not but consider these circumstances of my reception and introduction as a prelude to future advantages. The pleasing transactions of the day exhilarated my spirits; I evidently perceived a prepossession in my behalf; I exerted my utmost to improve the favorable impression and retired to rest with a serenity to which I had been long unaccustomed.

A ship in the road is preparing to sail. I have not time to add more. *You* know where remembrances are due, and will impart them. The first vessel that arrives from England will, I trust, convey pleasing intelligence of the welfare of my family and of yourself. Under all the eventful circumstances of life, be assured I shall remain unalterably yours.

LETTER II

Annapolis, October 1, 1769

Previous to the receipt of your letter the painful information had arrived that Powell[1] was no more! He was the valued friend of my early youth, and I shall ever cherish his remembrance with unabated attachment. To mention his professional excellence is unnecessary, the unanimous voice of the public having firmly established his superior pretensions. Nor need I express my fears that it is improbable we shall quickly "look upon his like again"; for how seldom is it that the great requisites of acting are so united in one man, as they were in him! Great however as his loss is to the public, it is still greater to his friends; to those who knew as we did his mild and amiable manners, his easy and unaffected vivacity, and his uniform candor and benevolence. My feelings on hearing of his death were much augmented by the particulars of a circumstance immediately preceding it: after having contended several days with the violence of his disorder, nature appeared totally exhausted, and he had lain for a considerable time with scarce a symptom of existence. His surrounding friends had mournfully yielded him to his fate and were expecting each moment the last convulsive exertion! when suddenly starting, with wonderful expression in his countenance, he repeated the speech in Macbeth commencing with the words: "Is this a dagger —— ," tracing with his eye the imaginary move-

---

[1] William Powell (1735-1769), a leading actor on the London stage from 1763 until his premature death.

ment of the delusive phantom; then a short period of recollection took place — he appeared conscious of having been under the influence of a delirium — invoked Heaven for mercy, and sunk lifeless on his pillow! What a strong instance of the ruling passion in his final exit! In him I have lost a faithful, animated friend; and "friends grow not thick on every bough." But no more of this — I will endeavor to relieve my mind from the intrusion of melancholy ideas by attempting to gratify your curiosity respecting this place and its environs.

Annapolis is nearly encompassed by the river Severn, and with every advantage of situation is built on a very irregular plan. The adjacent country presents a variety of beautiful prospects, agreeably diversified with well settled plantations, lofty woods, and navigable waters. In our little metropolis the public buildings do not impress the mind with any idea of magnificence, having been chiefly erected during the infancy of the colony when convenience was the directing principle without attention to the embellishment of art.

The courthouse,[2] situated on an eminence at the back of the town, commands a variety of views highly interesting, the entrance of the Severn, the majestic Chesapeake, and the eastern shore of Maryland being all united in one resplendent assemblage. Vessels of various sizes and figures are continually floating before the eye, which, while they add to the beauty of the scene, excite ideas of the most pleasing nature.

In the courthouse, the representatives of the people assemble for the dispatch of provincial business. The courts of justice are also held here; and here, likewise, the public offices are established. This building has nothing in its appearance expressive of the great purposes to which it is

[2] By "courthouse" Eddis means the State House or provincial capitol building.

appropriated; and by a strange neglect is suffered to fall continually into decay; being, both without and within, an emblem of public poverty, and at the same time a severe reflection on the government of this country, which, it seems, is considerably richer than the generality of the American provinces.

The council chamber is a detached building, adjacent to the former, on a very humble scale. It contains one tolerable room for the reception of the governor and his council, who meet here during the sitting of the assembly, and whose concurrence is necessary in passing all laws.

I am not yet enabled, from my own observation, to form any accurate judgment respecting the political disposition of the colonists; but if the information I have received may be relied on, they attend with a jealous eye to the conduct of their respective governors and to every regulation in the parent state which relates to their external or internal interests. In the northern provinces a republican spirit evidently prevails; and in the middle and southern they are, perhaps, too ready in taking the alarm whenever they conceive any measures are in agitation which may lessen their importance, embarrass their trade, or render them more dependent on the mother country. Almost from the commencement of their settlements they have occasionally combated against real or supposed innovations; and I am persuaded, whenever they become populous in proportion to the extent of their territory, they cannot be retained as British subjects otherwise than by inclination and interest. But I am wandering into a wide, unpleasing field of political disquisition, instead of pursuing the more agreeable path of description.

The governor's house is most beautifully situated, and when the necessary alterations are completed it will be a regular, convenient, and elegant building. The garden is not extensive, but it is disposed to the utmost advantage; the center walk is terminated by a small green mount, close to which the Severn approaches; this elevation commands an extensive view of the bay and the adjacent country. The same objects appear to equal advantage from the saloon and many apartments in the house; and perhaps I may be justified in asserting that there are but few mansions in the most rich and cultivated parts of England which are adorned with such splendid and romantic scenery.

The buildings in Annapolis were formerly of small dimensions and of an inelegant construction; but there are now several modern edifices which make a good appearance. There are few habitations without gardens, some of which are planted in a decent style and are well stocked.

At present, this city has more the appearance of an agreeable village than the metropolis of an opulent province, as it contains within its limits a number of small fields, which are intended for future erections. But in a few years it will probably be one of the best built cities in America, as a spirit of improvement is predominant and the situation is allowed to be equally healthy and pleasant with any on this side the Atlantic.

There is not, however, any probability that Annapolis will ever attain any importance in a commercial point of view: the harbor is not capable of containing many vessels of considerable burden; and the hazard of being frozen up for a long period during winter is a powerful obstacle to mercantile purposes. It is, however, the seat of government; the public offices are here established; and as many of the principal families have chosen this place for their residence, there are few towns of the same size in any part of the British dominions that can boast a more polished society.

You cannot travel any considerable distance in this country without crossing rivers, many of them wider than the Thames at Woolwich. Over these regular ferries are established at the charge of the respective counties; but though every proper method is adopted for expedition, yet such a number of considerable waters unavoidably occasion great delay.

In the vicinity of Annapolis are many pleasant villas, whose proprietors are eminent for their hospitality. Colonel Sharpe, the late governor,[3] possesses a most delightful retirement about seven miles distant; his house is on a large scale, the design is excellent, and the apartments well fitted up and perfectly convenient. The adjacent grounds are so judiciously disposed that utility and taste are everywhere happily united; and when the worthy owner has completed his extensive plan, Whitehall will be one of the most desirable situations in this or in any of the neighboring provinces.[4]

Colonel Sharpe has resided many years in this country, where he has established a reputation which reflects the highest honor on his public capacity and on his private virtues. This gentleman does not seem to entertain any idea of returning to his native land, but appears inclined to spend the residue of his days within the limits of a province which he has so long governed with honor to himself, satisfaction to the people, and fidelity to his soverign.

Annapolis, October 19th

I have lately made an excursion to the eastern shore of this province. As the narrative may possibly afford you some entertainment, I shall here endeavor to give you an account of the particulars of our journey.

[3] Horatio Sharpe (1718-1790), governor of Maryland, 1753-1769.
[4] Whitehall, a gem of Georgian style, stands on Whitehall Creek, just off the bay, in an excellent state of preservation. For the history of his mansion see Charles Scarlett, Jr., "Governor Horatio Sharpe's Whitehall," *Maryland Historical Magazine,* 44 (1951), 8-26.

On the thirteenth instant, the governor and his lady, with a party of gentlemen, amongst whom I had the honor to be included, embarked on board a vessel properly accommodated for our reception; the weather was remarkably fine, and a pleasant gale wafted us in about five hours to the seat of Mr. C[halmers].[5]

This gentleman resides on an island in the Chesapeake, about seven miles in length and of different breadth; the whole of which, being his entire property, is well cultivated, and produces great quantities of tobacco, grain, cattle, and stock of various kinds; and as it abounds likewise with game, the worthy proprietor lives in a manner independent of mankind, the monarch of his little fertile territory.

Early on the following morning, several of the neighboring gentry visited the island to pay their respects to the governor, and invitations poured in from every quarter. We were, however, under the necessity of declining these proofs of attention, His Excellency being obliged, on the sixteenth, to attend some provincial concerns in Annapolis. Accordingly, after partaking of a substantial breakfast in the true American style, which consisted not only of tea, coffee, and the usual accompaniments, but likewise of ham, dried venison, beef, and other relishing articles, we took leave of our friendly host, ferried over from his island to the main land, where carriages were waiting for our accommodation, and proceeded about twenty miles along the banks of the Chesapeake.

In the course of this little tour we passed several plantations, which not only proclaimed the opulence but the taste of their owners. About noon we arrived opposite Kent Island, which on that side is only divided by a narrow stream from the main land; we were quickly conveyed to the op-

[5] James Chalmers (d. 1806), later a Loyalist; author of *Plain Truth,* a reply to Paine's *Common Sense;* commander of the Maryland Loyalist Regiment during the War for Independence.

posite shore, and in a short time came to the house of Mr. H. where we enjoyed a cheerful evening; and on the following day embarked for the seat of government.

Kent Island is a narrow tract of land, about twenty miles in length, fertile, and well settled; many of the inhabitants possessing not only the comforts but the elegancies of life. This delectable spot forms one parish, the clerical emoluments of which afford a comfortable, if not an affluent subsistence to the incumbent. Kent Island ranges along the bay, at the distance of about ten miles from the western shore, and beautifully terminates a most delightful prospect highly variegated with wood and water.

As you cannot but be solicitous concerning my views and expectations, you will be glad to learn that they are highly favorable. In England there are few, even in great departments of the state, who possess so extensive a patronage as the governor of Maryland; and I am perfectly assured that his inclination to promote my interest is in full proportion to his ability. But public affairs do not, at this juncture, wear the most flattering aspect. You who know with what applause the repeal of the stamp act was received on this side the Atlantic, will not be surprised to hear that a revival of the claim of taxation, by laying duties on other articles, has renewed the apprehensions and discontents which had happily subsided; and the establishment of admiralty courts during the course of the preceding year appears to have raised a determined opposition to the proceedings of government. To know where it will terminate is beyond the reach of human penetration. Associations are forming from one extremity of this continent to the other; few appear to dissent from the popular creed; and it seems to be generally admitted that if the Americans steadily adhere to their non-importation agreement they will from the interest, if not from the equity, of the parent state, obtain redress of grievances. "Statist I am none, nor like to be"; therefore am by no means competent to deliver my sentiments on this very alarming subject. There are some zealots who are frantic enough to affect a bold language, and to talk of hostile measures if arguments and pacific remonstrances should prove ineffectual; but such men are deservedly treated with contempt by the wise and dispassionate. I am persuaded the principal persons in every government are not inclined to adopt any measures but what are founded on rectitude and moderation, from a settled belief that calm and respectful applications from the legislative body will eventually be productive of every desired consequence.

But enough of politics. I am looking forward with impatience to the day which will restore me to those who must participate in my good or evil fortune. Adieu!

LETTER III

Annapolis, January 15, 1770

Colonel F[itzhugh],[1] a gentleman of considerable property and a member of the council, early in December engaged the governor, with a circle of select friends, to pass a few days during the Christmas vacation at his seat in Calvert County, about seventy miles distant from Annapolis. Having the honor to be included in the party, I embarked on the twenty-second with the colonel on board a schooner which he had fitted up for occasional excursions; and considering the season of the year, we had a pleasant run to the place of our destination, which is delightfully situated within view of the Chesapeake, on the fertile banks of the river Patuxent.

Rousby Hall, which is the name of my friend's hospitable mansion, is as well known to the weary indigent traveler as to the affluent guest. In a country where hospitality is the distinguishing feature, the benevolent owner has established a preeminence which places his character in an exalted point of view.

The governor, on account of some particular engagements, did not quit Annapolis till the twenty-sixth; and on the thirtieth I accompanied Colonel Fitzhugh to the habitation of a gentleman, about twenty miles distant, where by appointment we met His Excellency with a numerous party

[1] Colonel William Fitzhugh (d. 1798) of Rousby Hall, Calvert County, was a member of the council, commissary general, and treasurer of the western shore. Rousby Hall was burned by the British in the War of 1812.

who had assembled to bid him welcome. All the good things of a plentiful country decorated the table of our munificent host; the wines were excellent and various; and cheerful blazing fires, with enlivening conversation, exhilarated the spirits, and rendered us totally regardless of the rigor of an American winter. On the ensuing day, the whole company proceeded to Rousby Hall, where we continued, in the full enjoyment of genuine hospitality, till the third instant; and it was with the utmost reluctance we were then permitted to take our departure.

Since we quitted Colonel Fitzhugh, we have visited most of the principal families in Calvert, St. Mary's, Charles, Prince George's, and Anne Arundel Counties;[2] and were everywhere received with the most obliging proofs of regard and attention. From the severity of the weather we occasionally encountered some hardships and inconveniences, but we were amply compensated at the end of every stage by excellent accommodations and sumptuous fare. Notwithstanding the dreary season, the eye was gratified with many picturesque and noble objects: we traveled a considerable way on the banks of the great river Potomac, which separates Maryland from Virginia; and though this country is greatly inferior in its present state to the highly cultivated parts of South Britain, yet on the whole it is well settled; the generality of the plantations are disposed with the utmost regularity, and in very many of the habitations we found elegance as well as comfort.

We passed an agreeable evening with a family nearly opposite to Alexandria in Virginia; and, had the weather been moderate, intended to have crossed the river on a visit to Major Washington,[3] who, as you may recollect, particu-

---

[2] These five southern counties of the western shore were the old settled area, studded with country seats where the first families lived.

[3] George Washington was at home to the Maryland gentry whom he knew from his regular visits to the Annapolis balls and theatre.

larly distinguished himself in the transactions of the late war; this gentleman has a pleasant seat on the banks of the Potomac, in the vicinity of the above town, which is named Mount Vernon, where he resides in full possession of universal love and esteem.

Yesterday we returned safe to Annapolis, greatly satisfied with our expedition.

February 20

On Saturday last our little city appeared in all its splendor. It was the anniversary of the proprietary's birth. The governor gave a grand entertainment on the occasion to a numerous party; the company brought with them every disposition to render each other happy; and the festivity concluded with cards and dancing, which engaged the attention of their respective votaries till an early hour.

I am persuaded there is not a town in England of the same size as Annapolis which can boast a greater number of fashionable and handsome women; and were I not satisfied to the contrary, I should suppose that the majority of our belles possessed every advantage of a long and familiar intercourfe with the manners and habits of your great metropolis.

I am told that beauty in this country is not of long duration: it is also asserted that in general the men do not possess such good stamina as the natives of Great Britain. Though every way equal in genius and enterprise, they are supposed less able to support fatigue, and to encounter the hardships of laborious employments.

During the winter there are assemblies every fortnight; the room for dancing is large; the construction elegant; and the whole illuminated to great advantage. At each extremity are apartments for the card tables, where select companies enjoy the circulation of the party-colored gentry without having their attention diverted by the sound of fiddles and the evolutions of youthful performers.

About Christmas an intense frost set in, which has continued till a few days since with unremitting severity. Our principal rivers for several weeks have been passable for carriages heavily laden; and in particular situations, innumerable skaters have exhibited on the glassy surface their feats of dexterity.

It is certainly extraordinary that in a latitude nearly parallel with Gilbraltar the inhabitants should experience, for a considerable duration, a degree of cold to which the northern extremities of the British Islands have never been accustomed; this, I am informed, proceeds entirely from local circumstances; the winds, prevalent in winter, blowing over those immense lakes situated to the westward of this and some neighboring provinces, impregnate the air with frigid particles that make us sensible of an inclemency equal to that experienced by the shivering Laplander.

In this country a heavy snow generally precedes the frost, during the continuance of which the atmosphere is beautifully serene, without any of those pernicious fogs so prevalent in your humid climate.

Notwithstanding the extensive forests that abound throughout this vast continent, fuel is an expensive article in all the considerable towns: provisions are in general cheap, but the price of labor is high, from which circumstance firing is comparatively dear, even on the most economical plan. I am, however, persuaded that by prudent management a respectable appearance may be supported in Maryland on terms infinitely more reasonable than in most parts of the mother country; and that greater opportunities are afforded to the industrious and enterprising to lay the foundation of a comfortable provision for a succeeding generation.

I am, etc.

LETTER IV

Annapolis, April 2, 1770

I thank you, my friend, for your very warm congratulations on my present happy and promising establishment. The scene is indeed, reversed; the remembrance of former disappointments tends but to excite a grateful sensibility of that providential goodness which has safely conducted me through a maze of difficulties and embarrassments, restored me to all the blessings of domestic peace, and apparently placed me in a situation that has little to fear from a reverse of fortune.

You have been rightly informed respecting the conduct of our worthy governor. From every observation I have hitherto been enabled to make, he appears perfectly competent to the discharge of his important duty. Not only in the summer, but during the extreme rigor of an American winter, it is his custom to rise early; till the hour of dinner he devotes the whole of his time to provincial concerns; the meanest individual obtains an easy and immediate access to his person; he investigates with accuracy the complicated duties of his station; and discovers, upon every occasion, alacrity in the dispatch of business, and a perfect knowledge of the relative connections of the country.

Had he been appointed to succeed a person who had consulted his private advantage in preference to that of the public, who had been found unequal to the discharge of his important trust, or remiss in the execution, it would have required no extraordinary exertion of abilities to have ap-

peared in a favorable point of view. But his immediate predecessor, by the invariable rectitude of his conduct, the affability of his manners, and his unremitting attention to the
happiness and prosperity of Maryland, had established a
well merited popularity, which during an administration of
sixteen years continued in full force, and has secured to him
the unabated love and attachment of a grateful people.

That our present supreme magistrate possesses an extensive capacity for government is indeed obvious to the most
superficial observer; but it may be objected that experience
is yet wanting to confirm his claim to eminent distinction. I
admit the force of the objection, and will likewise acknowledge the influence of partiality. He is my patron! my benefactor! I may possibly be animated by the impulse of gratitude to delineate his conduct in the strongest colors. To
time I therefore leave him, the only true criterion by which
any character can be properly established. To that incontest-
able decision he himself emphatically appeals in the conclusion of his first speech to the general assembly of the
province. Let me quote a declaration which, should he be
found defective, will stand recorded to his disadvantage, and
likewise prove that I have seen through a false medium and
have been too precipitate in drawing conclusions.

Gentlemen of both Houses,

I am sensible that I shall be judged of by my actions, and not
by any assurances I may now give you of my future conduct. To
that test I most readily submit, and shall be truly happy, when
I leave you, to be able, like my predecessor, to lay my hand on
my heart, in confidence of having acted solely on the principles
here laid down; and of having merited, by so doing, the thanks
of those over whom I have the honor to preside.

Maryland is a proprietary government, and owes its original settlement to religious motives. In the year 1632, Lord

Baltimore, who then possessed considerable influence, obtained a grant of this country from Charles the First, until which time it had been considered as a part of Virginia.* The Roman Catholics were at that period greatly harassed by the Puritans, who were then beginning to become the predominant party; and to secure them an asylum where they might safely profess their religious tenets was the motive which induced the above nobleman to solicit the grant. Accordingly, in the following year about two hundred families of that persuasion, some of whom were of considerable distinction, embarked from Ireland for this newly acquired territory, where they were favorably received by the Indian inhabitants, whose affection they had the good fortune to conciliate by the liberality of their conduct; insomuch that they were soon enabled to purchase extensive tracts on the most moderate terms, and to settle their lands to the best advantage without entertaining any anxious apprehensions from the original possessors.

During the existence of that illegal power, which had subverted the ancient constitution both in church and state, the proprietor of Maryland was deprived of his authority and his property; and a governor appointed by the protector was substituted in his stead: but at the restoration the property of the province reverted to its natural possessor; Lord Baltimore was reinstated in his privileges, and quickly demonstrated by his distinguished conduct that he had every claim which merit and justice could afford. He instituted a perfect toleration with respect to religion. He gave the utmost encouragement to agriculture and to commerce. In consequence of his judicious exertions, the colony increased rapidly in wealth and population, and persons of all denominations, attracted by the moderation and equity of his

* The royal grant was given on this singular condition, that the proprietary should annually present at Windsor Castle two Indian arrows.

government, were emulous to obtain settlements under so flourishing and respectable an establishment.

At the demise of Charles the Second, a weak, arbitrary, and tyrannical monarch succeeded to the throne; during whose short but pernicious administration this noble family were again deprived of their possession, which had been derived from royal bounty and had been wonderfully improved at the expense of infinite labor and proportionable disbursements.[1] They were, however, again reinstated, in consequence of that glorious revolution which established the British constitution on a firm unalterable basis.

Though by this ever memorable event the proprietor was restored to the profits of the government, yet the right of governing could not consistently under the new system be conferred on a Roman Catholic; therefore, until the family renounced that communion, the Crown assumed the power of appointing the supreme magistrate.

Lord Baltimore, the present proprietor, has a right to exercise in his own person all the executive offices of government; and in his absence to nominate one to that department with the consent and approbation of his majesty.

The present governor, who married his eldest sister, was elevated to that situation a few months before my arrival in the country.

Maryland is divided into fourteen counties, seven on the western and seven on the eastern side of the bay, each of which sends four representatives to the general assembly. The city of Annapolis has likewise the privilege of delegating two. These gentlemen form the lower house, and, if I

---

[1] Eddis gives a somewhat misleading impression of proprietary losses. The Lords Baltimore never lost their real property rights in Maryland until the American Revolution cut them off altogether. Twice they were deprived of their governmental authority: once during the interregnum and later during the twenty-five years following the Glorious Revolution.

may compare small things to great, possess similar powers with the commons in the British parliament. The council is composed of ten members, who are nominated by the governor: they have the appellation of Honorable, and with them he is to advise in all matters respecting the general interests of the community. During the sitting of the assembly they become a superior branch of the legislature, and their confirmation is essential to the passing of all laws.

The governor is in every particular the representative of the Crown. He appoints the time for the sitting of both houses; his assent is necessary for the confirmation of their proceedings; and he prorogues or dissolves them, as appears to him most consistent with the authority of government, and the interests of the people.

I have previously observed that Maryland was originally settled by a colony of Roman Catholics who emigrated from Ireland early in the last century under the patronage of the then Lord Baltimore. For some time the inhabitants of that persuasion maintained the entire ascendancy;[2] but their numbers are at present very inconsiderable, and their influence of no weight in the public concerns of the province. They, however, continue to be tolerated, without being permitted to participate in the offices of government. The established religion is that of the church of England, the members of which communion very greatly exceed the aggregate body of the dissenters of every denomination.

The province is divided into forty-four parishes, many of which are populous and extensive. The patronage is solely vested in the governor, who is thereby enabled to provide in an ample manner for many worthy and respectable characters; and when all circumstances are taken into consideration, the clergy in this part of the world will be found to

---

[2] Doubtless Roman Catholics maintained the ascendancy until 1688, but doubtless, too, they were numerically in the minority from the beginning; certainly after 1650 they were a decided minority.

possess advantages greatly superior to the generality of their brethren in the mother country. Pluralities have never been admitted, the colonists being universally prepossessed against that practice; and to attempt such an innovation would excite ferments of a dangerous nature. Each incumbent has a neat and convenient habitation, with a sufficient quantity of land in proper cultivation to answer every useful and domestic purpose; and the emoluments arising from the least beneficial preferment are amply sufficient to support an appearance perfectly consistent with the respectability of the clerical profession. The holders of church benefices are also happily exempted from the frequent altercations which unavoidably take place in the mother country on account of the collection of tithes.

By the laws of this province, all public dues are levied by a poll tax. The clergy, from this provision, are entitled to forty pounds of tobacco for every person within a limited age, at the rate of twelve shillings and sixpence the hundred weight. Persons who plant tobacco have it in their option to pay either in money or in produce; those who do not are constantly assessed in specie. A list of the taxables, properly authenticated, is delivered to the sheriff of each county, who collects the clerical revenues with other public claims, and deducting a moderate commission for transacting this concern, the residue is paid with regularity and dispatch to the respective incumbents.

As the emoluments of benefices increase in proportion to the increase of inhabitants, many benefices in this government are rapidly advancing in value, and must before many years elapse very greatly exceed the present annual amount. Frederick County, which is considerably the most extensive in this province in its present state, is only divided into two parishes, one of which, denominated All Saints, I am credibly informed is at this period estimated at full one thousand pounds sterling *per annum;* and from the great increase of population, which is daily taking place in that beautiful and fertile country, it will very probably soon produce an income little inferior to many English bishoprics.[3]

I cannot conceive on what principle the colonists are so strongly prejudiced against the introduction of the episcopal order: such an establishment would assuredly be attended with many local advantages, and save much trouble and expense to gentlemen educated in America for the sacred function who, on the present system, are under the necessity of taking a voyage to England for the purpose of ordination. Throughout the southern provinces the members of the established church greatly exceed those of all other denominations; yet I am persuaded any attempt to establish an hierarchy would be resisted with as much acrimony as during the gloomy prevalence of puritanical zeal. This spirit of opposition, to a measure so evidently conducive to the general good, is the more extraordinary, as the inhabitants of this part of America discover on every possible occasion an enlarged and liberal disposition. They have, however, conceived such rooted prejudices against the higher orders of the church that they are positively persuaded the advantages to be acquired by such an institution in the colonies would by no means counterbalance the evils which might arise from it.*

[3] Eddis had been correctly informed, incredible as it seems. All Saints Parish was therefore a plum in the Lord Proprietor's gift. But the parish seethed with discontent which boiled over when Frederick, Lord Baltimore presented his worthless sycophant, Bennet Allen, to the living. Communicants of All Saints had hoped to have the gigantic parish divided. This tragi-comedy is told in all its color by Josephine Fisher, "Bennet Allen, Fighting Parson," *Maryland Historical Magazine,* 38 (1943), 299-322 and 39 (1944), 49-72.

* The establishment of episcopacy in America, since the conclusion of the war, is among those very extraordinary circumstances which cannot be accounted for by human penetration.

While the colonies were a part of the British empire, the introduction of dignitaries was opposed with a most determined spirit, from an opinion

In a political point of view, independent of religious motives, it is much to be lamented that a plan of this nature was not determined on before the colonies had arrived to their present degree of population and consequence: had an order of nobility been created, and dignitaries in the church appointed at an early period, it would most assuredly have greatly tended to cherish a steady adherence to monarchical principles, and have more strongly riveted the attachment of the colonies to the parent state. Inattention to principles of such importance has gradually given birth to sentiments

---

generally conceived that the powers they would be authorised to exercise might eventually be subversive of freedom; but when they were entirely at liberty to adopt any regulations for ecclesiastical government, totally independent of the mother country, they voluntarily and unanimously solicited the consecration of bishops.

About three years since, two clergymen, one from New York and the other from Philadelphia, arrived in England and received episcopal consecration. An act of Parliament had previously passed, for the purpose of dispensing with the oaths to the British government, in the case of those gentlemen, and in all similar cases. They were properly recommended hither by a convention of the clergy in the United States of America; and another of their brethren, sanctioned in like manner from Virginia, has been lately consecrated here as bishop for that state under the forementioned authority. So that there are three bishops now in that country, who will have full power to continue the uninterrupted succession which has existed from the days of the apostles; not to mention a gentleman who, a considerable time before the others, had been consecrated by the nonjuring bishops in Scotland, and who resides in Connecticut. None of these, however, have any fixed income, but depend upon the voluntary contributions of their respective congregations, to whom they regularly preach on Sundays and officiate as parish priests. They have the title of *Right Reverend,* but have no particular powers, except that of ordaining deacons and priests and superintending the religious and moral conduct of the clergy, who are, in some sort, rendered accountable to them. It is, I believe, generally allowed that the members of the episcopal church increase throughout all the States, beyond any other denomination, although they are nearly upon an equality with the others, respecting the privileges from the civil power. In British America there is a bishop, chiefly resident in Nova Scotia, who has much the same distinction with those already particularized, but enjoys an established salary of about eleven hundred pounds sterling a year.

totally repugnant to the genius of our most excellent constitution. A republican spirit appears generally to predominate; and it will undoubtedly require the utmost exertion of legislative wisdom to establish on a permanent basis the future political and commercial connection between Great Britain and America.

There are many discerning and intelligent persons who are decidedly of opinion that the acquisition of Canada is highly prejudicial to the interests of the mother country. The Americans are, by this event, relieved from continual apprehensions; their frontiers are no longer exposed to the incursions of a restless enterprising neighbor; and they begin to encourage ideas of self-importance, which have been wonderfully promoted by the success attending their recent opposition to the operation of the stamp duties.

Had Canada still continued annexed to the French empire, it is evident that the British provinces, from a well-grounded dread of such numerous and powerful opponents, must unavoidably, on a principle of self-preservation if not of affection, have remained firmly and indissolubly attached to the parent state; a just apprehension of real calamities would have operated with efficacy against imaginary evils; and the natural and constitutional-dependence of the colonies on the protection and assistance of Great Britain would have promoted a constant and mutual interchange of friendly and benevolent offices, which must have settled the union on a permanent foundation and on terms reciprocally honorable and advantageous to both countries.

What will be the event of the present discontents which, I am truly concerned to observe, are universally predominant, time alone can determine. There are amongst us many restless spirits, who are evidently industrious in fomenting divisions and exciting jealousies; and unless wise and constitutional measures are immediately adopted, there is too much reason to apprehend consequences of a serious and alarming nature.

You will think, and with great justice, that I have ventured far beyond my depth in presuming to descant on such important topics; but remember it was you who started the game; I have only, like an unskilful rider, followed an irresistible impulse, and if I retain but my seat on the saddle I shall be amply satisfied.

Adieu! etc.

LETTER V

Though we are yet far behind the mother country with respect to cultivation and improvements, yet, in a comparative view Maryland may boast considerable advantages. The inhabitants are enterprising and industrious; commerce and agriculture are encouraged; and every circumstance clearly evinces that this colony is making a rapid progress to wealth, power, and population.

Provisions of every kind are excellent and plentiful; and the Chesapeake, with our numerous rivers, affords a surprising variety of excellent fish. Poultry and wild fowl abound amongst the humble cottagers; and beef, mutton, pork, and other provisions are at least equal to the production of the best British markets.

Deer a few years since were very numerous in the interior settlements; but from the unfair methods adopted by the hunters their numbers are exceedingly diminished. These people, whose only motive was to procure the hide of the animal, were dexterous, during the winter season, in tracing their path through the snow; and from the animal's incapacity to exert speed under such circumstances, great multitudes of them were annually slaughtered and their carcasses left in the woods. This practice, however, has been thought worthy the attention of the legislature, and an act of assembly has taken place, laying severe penalties on "persons detected in pursuing or destroying deer, within a limited term"; and it is probable the apprehension of punishment

may very greatly restrain if not totally eradicate an evil
founded on cruelty and rapacity.

In England, almost every county is distinguished by a
peculiar dialect; even different habits and different modes of
thinking evidently discriminate inhabitants, whose local situation is not far remote; but in Maryland and throughout
the adjacent provinces, it is worthy of observation that a
striking similarity of speech universally prevails; and it is
strictly true that the pronunciation of the generality of the
people has an accuracy and elegance that cannot fail of grat-
ifying the most judicious ear.

The colonists are composed of adventurers, not only from
every district of Great Britain and Ireland, but from almost
every other European government where the principles of
liberty and commerce have operated with spirit and efficacy.
Is it not, therefore, reasonable to suppose that the English
language must be greatly corrupted by such a strange inter-
mixture of various nations? The reverse is, however, true.
The language of the immediate descendants of such a pro-
miscuous ancestry is perfectly uniform and unadulterated;
nor has it borrowed any provincial or national accent from
its British or foreign parentage.

For my part, I confess myself totally at a loss to account
for the apparent difference between the colonists and persons under equal circumstances of education and fortune
resident in the mother country. This uniformity of language
prevails not only on the coast, where Europeans form a considerable mass of the people, but likewise in the interior
parts, where population has made but slow advances, and
where opportunities seldom occur to derive any great advantages from an intercourse with intelligent strangers.

You, my friend, are seated at the fountainhead of literary
and political intelligence, and from you I shall expect frequent and circumstantial communications. Most sincerely
do I wish you may be enabled to acquaint me that the first

transaction in the ensuing sessions of parliament is a total repeal of acts which are never likely to be productive of any considerable revenue; and which are esteemed in this country to have no other tendency but to enforce claims which the colonists universally consider as impolitic and unconstitutional. How far their sentiments are justly founded, I am by no means competent to determine; but it is a certain fact that the statute imposing duties on glass, paper, and tea[1] has undermined the foundation of that cordiality, which the repeal of the stamp act had happily reestablished; and it is with the utmost concern, I am necessitated to acquaint you that a spirit of discontent and opposition is universally predominant in the colonies.

Annapolis, June 14th

I am sure you will take a sincere part in the happiness I now experience. My wife and son arrived yesterday from England, and I am again restored to the blessings of domestic life. With their affectionate wishes, believe me, etc.

[1] In 1767 parliament had revived American opposition by levying duties on tea, glass, paper, and painter's colors imported into the colonies, the Townshend Acts. When Eddis wrote the duties had already been repealed though this intelligence took some time to reach Annapolis.

LETTER VI

Annapolis, September 20, 1770

Your information relative to the situation of servants in this country is far from being well founded. I have now been upwards of twelve months resident in Maryland, and am thereby enabled to convey to you a tolerable idea on this subject.

Persons in a state of servitude are under four distinct denominations: negroes, who are the entire property of their respective owners; convicts, who are transported from the mother country for a limited term; indented servants, who are engaged for five years previous to their leaving England; and free-willers, who are supposed, from their situation, to possess superior advantages.

The negroes in this province are, in general, natives of the country, very few in proportion being imported from the coast of Africa. They are better clothed, better fed, and better treated, than their unfortunate brethren, whom a more rigid fate hath subjected to slavery in our West India islands; neither are their employments so laborious, nor the acts of the legislature so partially oppressive against them. The further we proceed to the northward, the less number of people are to be found of this complexion. In the New England government, negroes are almost as scarce as on your side of the Atlantic, and but few are under actual slavery; but as we advance to the south, their multitudes astonish-

35

ingly increase, and in the Carolinas they considerably exceed the number of white inhabitants.*

Maryland is the only province into which convicts may be freely imported. The Virginians have inflicted very severe penalties on any masters of vessels, or others, who may attempt to introduce persons under this description into their colony. They have been influenced in this measure by an apprehension that, from the admission of such inmates into their families, the prevalence of bad example might tend to universal depravity, in spite of every regulation and restraining law.

Persons convicted of felony and in consequence transported to this continent, if they are able to pay the expense of passage, are free to pursue their fortune agreeably to their inclinations or abilities. Few, however, have means to avail themselves of this advantage. These unhappy beings are, generally, consigned to an agent, who classes them suitably to their real or supposed qualifications; advertises them for sale, and disposes of them, for seven years, to planters, to mechanics, and to such as choose to retain them for domestic service. Those who survive the term of servitude seldom establish their residence in this country: the stamp of infamy

---

* Notwithstanding the climate of North America is less favorable to the constitution of negroes than the European settlements in the torrid zone, they nevertheless increase rapidly in almost every part of that extensive continent. The last importation of slaves into Maryland was, as I am credibly informed, in the year 1769; and though great losses have been sustained in consequence of the war, and desertions to the British standard, their numbers are at least doubled since that time, without any foreign supply. To account for a circumstance apparently so improbable, it must be observed that on the American continent the planters generally adopted a more liberal mode in their African intercourse than has been pursued in the islands. They did not import slaves for the supply of foreign settlements, but purchased for their own immediate use, without any particular preference to either sex. The consequence is obvious: they have multiplied in a due proportion, and notwithstanding the occasional severity of the climate and the recent calamities of war, their numbers are fully sufficient for their respective occupations.

is too strong upon them to be easily erased; they either return to Europe and renew their former practices; or, if they
have fortunately imbibed habits of honesty and industry,
they remove to a distant situation, where they may hope to
remain unknown, and be enabled to pursue with credit every
possible method of becoming useful members of society.

In your frequent excursions about the great metropolis,
you cannot but observe numerous advertisements offering
the most seducing encouragement to adventurers under
every possible description; to those who are disgusted with
the frowns of fortune in their native land; and to those of an
enterprising disposition, who are tempted to court her smiles
in a distant region. These persons are referred to agents, or
crimps, who represent the advantages to be obtained in
America in colors so alluring that it is almost impossible to
resist their artifices. Unwary persons are accordingly induced to enter into articles, by which they engage to become
servants, agreeable to their respective qualifications, for the
term of five years; every necessary accommodation being
found them during the voyage; and every method taken
that they may be treated with tenderness and humanity during the period of servitude; at the expiration of which they
are taught to expect that opportunities will assuredly offer
to secure to the honest and industrious a competent provision for the remainder of their days.

The generality of the inhabitants in this province are very
little acquainted with those fallacious pretenses, by which
numbers are continually induced to embark for this continent. On the contrary, they too generally conceive an opinion that the difference is merely nominal between the indented servant and the convicted felon; nor will they readily
believe that people who had the least experience in life, and
whose characters were unexceptionable, would abandon
their friends and families and their ancient connections, for
a servile situation in a remote appendage to the British em-

pire. From this persuasion they rather consider the convict as the more profitable servant, his term being for seven, the latter only for five years; and, I am sorry to observe, that there are but few instances wherein they experience different treatment. Negroes being a property for life, the death of slaves, in the prime of youth or strength, is a material loss to the proprietor; they are, therefore, almost in every instance, under more comfortable circumstances than the miserable European, over whom the rigid planter exercises an inflexible severity. They are strained to the utmost to perform their allotted labor; and, from a prepossession in many cases too justly founded, they are supposed to be receiving only the just reward which is due to repeated offenses. There are doubtless many exceptions to this observation, yet, generally speaking, they groan beneath a worse than Egyptian bondage. By attempting to lighten the intolerable burthen, they often render it more insupportable. For real or imaginary causes, these frequently attempt to escape, but very few are successful; the country being intersected with rivers, and the utmost vigilance observed in detecting persons under suspicious circumstances who, when apprehended, are committed to close confinement, advertised, and delivered to their respective masters; the party who detects the vagrant being entitled to a reward. Other incidental charges arise. The unhappy culprit is doomed to a severe chastisement; and a prolongation of servitude is decreed in full proportion to expenses incurred and supposed inconveniences resulting from a desertion of duty.

The situation of the free-willer is, in almost every instance, more to be lamented than either that of the convict or the indented servant, the deception which is practiced on those of this description being attended with circumstances of greater duplicity and cruelty. Persons under this denomination are received under express conditions that on their arrival in America they are to be allowed a stipulated number of days to dispose of themselves to the greatest advantage. They are told that their services will be eagerly solicited in proportion to their abilities; that their reward will be adequate to the hazard they encounter by courting fortune in a distant region; and that the parties with whom they engage will readily advance the sum agreed on for their passage; which, being averaged at about nine pounds sterling, they will speedily be enabled to repay, and to enjoy, in a state of liberty, a comparative situation of ease and affluence.

With these pleasing ideas they support with cheerfulness the hardships to which they are subjected during the voyage; and, with the most anxious sensations of delight, approach the land which they consider as the scene of future prosperity. But scarce have they contemplated the diversified objects which naturally attract attention; scarce have they yielded to the pleasing reflection that every danger, every difficulty, is happily surmounted, before their fond hopes are cruelly blasted, and they find themselves involved in all the complicated miseries of a tedious, laborious, and unprofitable servitude.

Persons resident in America, being accustomed to procure servants for a very trifling consideration, under absolute terms for a limited period, are not often disposed to hire adventurers, who expect to be gratified in full proportion to their acknowledged qualifications; but, as they support authority with a rigid hand, they little regard the former situation of their unhappy dependants.

This disposition, which is almost universally prevalent, is well known to the parties who on your side of the Atlantic engage in this iniquitous and cruel commerce. It is therefore an article of agreement with these deluded victims that if they are not successful in obtaining situations on their own terms within a certain number of days after their arrival in the country, they are then to be sold, in order to defray the charges of passage, at the discretion of the master of the vessel or the agent to whom he is consigned in the province.

You are also to observe that servants imported, even under this favorable description, are rarely permitted to set their feet on shore until they have absolutely formed their respective engagements. As soon as the ship is stationed in her berth, planters, mechanics, and others, repair on board; the adventurers of both sexes are exposed to view, and very few are happy enough to make their own stipulations, some very extraordinary qualifications being absolutely requisite to obtain this distinction; and even when this is obtained, the advantages are by no means equivalent to their sanguine expectations. The residue, stung with disappointment and vexation, meet with horror the moment which dooms them, under an appearance of equity, to a limited term of slavery. Character is of little importance; their abilities not being found of a superior nature, they are sold as soon as their term of election is expired, apparel and provision being their only compensation; till, on the expiration of five tedious laborious years, they are restored to a dearly purchased freedom.

From this detail, I am persuaded you will no longer imagine that the servants in this country are in a better situation than those in Britain. You have heard of convicts who rather chose to undergo the severest penalties of the law than endure the hardships which are annexed to their situation during a state of servitude on this side the Atlantic. Indolence, accompanied with a train of vicious habits, has doubtless great influence on the determination of such unhappy wretches; but it is surely to be lamented that men whose characters are unblemished, whose views are founded on honest and industrious principles, should fall a sacrifice to avarice and delusion, and indiscriminately be blended with the most profligate and abandoned of mankind.

It seems astonishing that a circumstance so well known, particularly in this province, should not have been generally circulated through every part of the British empire. Were the particulars of this iniquitous traffic universally divulged, those who have established offices in London and in the principal seaports for the regular conduct of this business would be pointed out to obloquy, and their punishment would serve as a beacon to deter the ignorant and unwary from becoming victims to the insidious practices of avarice and deceit.

I am ready to admit there is every appearance of candor on the part of the agents and their accomplices. Previous to the embarkation of any person under the respective agreements, the parties regularly comply with the requisitions of a law wisely calculated to prevent clandestine transportation; they appear before a magistrate and give their voluntary assent to the obligations they have mutually entered into. But are not such adventurers induced to this measure in consequence of ignorance and misrepresentation? Assuredly they are. They are industriously taught to expect advantages infinitely superior to their most sanguine views in Britain. Every lucrative incentive is delineated in the most flattering colors; and they fondly expect to acquire that independence in the revolution of a few years which the longest life could not promise with the exertion of their best abilities in the bosom of their native country.

I will relieve your attention from this painful subject by relating an anecdote of an interesting nature, with which I became acquainted soon after my arrival in these parts.

A gentleman of considerable influence and fortune purchased a servant as an assistant to his gardener; having been previously informed that he had originally acted in that capacity and was qualified for the undertaking. The man, soon after he was brought on shore, received instructions to enter on his business, when it was immediately discovered that he was wholly unacquainted with the nature of his employment. On being interrogated relative to this deception, he acquainted his master that

extreme indigence induced him to abandon his native country — that in the course of the voyage, having intimated that he had not been brought up to any mechanical profession, he was informed by the captain it was absolutely necessary he should avow some particular calling, in order to secure a more comfortable situation; that in America a competent skill in gardening was easily attainable, and seldom required the exertion of greater talents than what were immediately essential for domestic purposes; and that by engaging in such employment he might avoid a more laborious servitude under the discipline of some rigid and inflexible planter.

This declaration was delivered in terms so apparently consistent with truth as obtained entire credit with his master, who from his deportment and exterior was likewise induced to form sentiments much to his advantage; he therefore determined to receive him into his family, in the capacity of a domestic, and to give him that encouragement to which he might be entitled by the propriety of his future conduct.

Every sentiment of gratitude appeared to operate on the mind of the servant when he found himself destined to a station more comfortable than his original allotment; and for some time the whole tenor of his actions was such as might show that he highly merited the indulgence which he had so unexpectedly obtained.

For a few months his diligence and attention secured him the entire approbation of his master, and he was continually gaining ground on his confidence and esteem. It was, therefore, with the utmost concern his benefactor began to observe an appearance of discontent, a disregard to the duties of his station, and an evident alteration in every particular. Remonstrances and threats were equally ineffectual: his disposition became sullen and reserved, while he obstinately refused to assign any cause for such an obvious change in his conduct. At length, he quitted the house of his benevolent employer, and by traveling in the night and lying concealed in the day, he took the proper precautions to elude the vigilance of pursuit.

His plan, though well concerted, was nevertheless ineffectual. In a few days he was discovered, almost famished. Necessity compelled him to supplicate the aid of charity: his story was equivocal and excited suspicion; he obtained relief but with the detention of his person. A magistrate before whom he was conveyed threatened him with confinement and rigorous treatment unless he gave a proper and satisfactory account from whence he came and the circumstances which had reduced him to his present situation. Finding every fallacious pretext fruitless, he made a candid and explicit discovery, and was, in consequence, with all possible expedition conducted to the presense of a master whose tenderness he had basely returned with such unpardonable ingratitude.

The most compassionate nature is seldom proof against repeated instances of an incorrigible disposition. It was therefore thought necessary that he should experience the consequences of his behavior, but he was previously reminded of the repeated acts of kindness that had been shown him and the ungrateful return he had made. From such considerations it was observed that it was a debt strictly due to justice to compel him to serve the residue of his time in the most laborious employment allotted to worthless servants. He was accordingly sentenced to the iron mines, there to reap the bitter effects of his conduct.

Overwhelmed with the consciousness of guilt and terrified at the prospect of the punishment that awaited him, the unfortunate culprit, in the most ingenuous terms, confessed the equity of the sentence passed upon him, but not without an intimation that there were circumstances in his case which, were they known, he was persuaded, would plead powerfully in his behalf. An irresistible inclination to return to his native country and the obstacles which appeared to bar his delusive hopes had possessed his mind with that gloom and discontent which had almost obliterated the impressions of gratitude, and occasioned that conduct which had brought him into his present situation. He concluded by declaring that he had not the most distant claim to compassion, yet relying on that goodness and lenity which he had so frequently abused, he was encouraged to admit a ray of hope and to supplicate forgiveness, however undeserved.

His humane master heard him with the most candid attention. He pitied a deviation from rectitude, which originated in motives natural to the human mind; and determined not only to exempt him from the situation to which he had been justly doomed, but to send him, by an early opportunity, to his much loved native country, there to pursue such eligible methods as Providence might suggest for his future comfortable provision. I shall not attempt to delineate the transports which on this intimation took possession of his mind.

About this time, the captain of a ship preparing to sail for England signified his want of a steward to attend on those passengers who had engaged his cabin for the voyage; the emancipated servant was recommended for this employment; his services were accepted; and with solemn assurances of the most lasting and grateful attachment, he bade farewell to a master by whose generous, disinterested conduct he was so providentially restored to happiness and to liberty.

Two years elapsed without the least intelligence respecting his situation, when, at length, a letter arrived, filled with every sentiment of gratitude.

His sense of repeated obligations was acknowledged in terms which delineated a heart conscious of the important benefits he had experienced; and he concluded by entreating his late master's acceptance of a bill, as a trifling consideration for the residue of that time, which he had been so generously and humanely exempted from serving.

The sum remitted very greatly exceeded the original cost of the most valuable servant. In this epistle not the least intimation was given relative to the circumstance which had enabled a man, so lately at the lowest ebb of misery, to spare from his immediate occasion so considerable a sum as *thirty pounds;* but an answer was requested, to be addressed to a merchant in London, that the party concerned might be properly apprised his bill was received and acknowledged.

Mr. J——— was inexpressibly happy in the pleasing reflection that, by an indulgence of lenity natural to his disposition, he had been rendered by Heaven the instrument of such unexpected prosperity. He could not for a moment admit the idea of appropriating any part of such money to himself, as the payment of a debt which he considered as a free donation to the claims of humanity; but he was naturally anxious to become acquainted with the particular events by which his late servant was so happily situated as to obtain the power of transmitting such a proof of his honesty and gratitude. He, therefore, immediately addressed a letter to the merchant, expressive of the

satisfaction he experienced in receiving intelligence of such an agreeable nature, and desiring him to return the note, which he had enclosed for that purpose, into the hands of the party who had conceived it his duty to transmit it, with earnest wishes that his future successes might amply compensate for every former calamity. He had only to request that by an early opportunity he would afford him the satisfaction of knowing by what unexpected circumstance he had been so rapidly and so providentially favored with the smiles of fortune.

By the return of the first ship, an answer from the agent arrived. The bill was sent back with an earnest entreaty that if Mr. J—— refused to apply it to his particular occasions he would appropriate it to some charitable purpose; that with respect to the situation of the man, formerly his servant, there were powerful reasons which precluded him from giving the information he requested. All that he was at liberty to disclose was that the person who had visited America, under circumstances so desperate and forlorn, who had been necessitated to become a common indented servant, subject to all the hardships and miseries incident to so abject a condition, was, by an astonishing transition of fortune, elevated to a very affluent and respectable situation in his native country.

The above particulars were delivered to me by the benevolent master himself, who during a course of years has assiduously endeavored, by every eligible mode of inquiry, to develop a secret so industriously concealed from his knowledge; but every method has hitherto proved ineffectual, and he has now relinquished the idea of having so natural a curiosity even confidentially gratified.

LETTER VII

You observe that, in the course of my correspondence, I have not particularly mentioned any towns of consequence within the limits of this government. In all probability, from the multitude of rivers which, with their branches, intersect this country in almost every direction, Maryland will never abound with ports or establishments of any considerable magnitude. By the advantage of so many navigable waters, an opportunity is afforded to ship the produce of many extensive districts, even at the doors of the respective planters, who consequently have not that inducement, common to most countries, for establishing themselves in populous communities.

Frederick County alone, from its interior situation, appears precluded from this benefit. But should a plan, now in agitation, to remove the obstructions in the great river Potomac, be attended with the desired consequences, that very fertile and extensive country will, in a great measure, participate in the advantages which are common to the other parts of the province.

On the arrival of Lord Baltimore, the original proprietor, with those families who had emigrated under the grant which he had obtained from the Crown, the first establishment was formed on the northern shore of the Potomac. The bounds of a town were ascertained; temporary habitations were erected; and this place, which was destined to be the seat of government, was distinguished by the name of

St. Mary's Town. But in process of time that situation at the southern extremity of the province was considered to be inconvenient for the dispatch of public business, and another spot more central was selected, which appeared to possess every possible advantage. Proper encouragement was given to promote population; a charter of incorporation was obtained; and the new metropolis, in honor of the then reigning monarch, received the appellation of Annapolis.

In a former letter I attempted to convey some idea of the truly picturesque and beautiful situation of our little capital. Several of the most opulent families have here established their residence; and hospitality is the characteristic of the inhabitants. Party prejudices have little influence on social intercourse: the grave and ancient enjoy the blessings of a respectable society, while the young and gay have various amusements to engage their hours of relaxation and to promote that mutual connection so essential to their future happiness.

You well know that I have ever been strongly attached to the rational entertainment resulting from theatrical exhibitions. When I bade farewell to England, I little expected that my passion for the drama could have been gratified in any tolerable degree at a distance so remote from the great mart of genius; and I brought with me strong prepossessions in behalf of favorite performers whose merits were fully established by the universal sanction of intelligent judges. My pleasure and my surprise were therefore excited in proportion on finding performers in this country equal at least to those who sustain the best of the first characters in your most celebrated provincial theatres. Our governor, from a strong conviction that the stage under proper regulations may be rendered of general utility and made subservient to the great interests of religion and virtue, patronises the American company; and as their present place of exhibition is on a small scale and inconveniently situated, a subscription by his example has been rapidly completed to erect a new theatre on a commodious if not an elegant plan. The manager is to deliver tickets for two seasons to the amount of the respective subscriptions, and it is imagined that the money which will be received at the doors from nonsubscribers will enable him to conduct the business without difficulty; and when the limited number of performances is completed, the entire property is to be vested in him. This will be a valuable addition to our catalog of amusements. The building is already in a state of forwardness, and the day of opening is anxiously expected. This circumstance has carried me inadvertently from my proper subject. Give me pardon for the digression. I will return into the road from which I deviated.

Annapolis, with every advantage to render it an agreeable residence, labors under inconveniences which will greatly impede its progress to commercial importance. The harbor, as I have formerly observed, is not sufficiently commodious for vessels of considerable burden; and the road is too much exposed to lade or unlade with safety or convenience. But the province has been amply compensated for this disappointment by the rise of a settlement which in the memory of many persons now in being has increased with the most astonishing rapidity, and promises, by an equal progress, to rank with the most populous and opulent establishments on this side the Atlantic.

This place, which is named Baltimore in compliment to the proprietary family, is situated on the northern branch of the river Patapsco, about thirty miles higher up the bay of Chesapeake than Annapolis, and at nearly the same distance by land. Within these few years some scattered cottages were only to be found on this spot, occupied by obscure storekeepers merely for the supply of the adjacent plantations. But the peculiar advantages it possesses with respect to the trade of the frontier counties of Virginia, Pennsylvania, and

Maryland, so strongly impressed the mind of Mr. John Stevenson, an Irish gentleman who had settled in the vicinity in a medical capacity, that he first conceived the important project of rendering this port the grand emporium of Maryland commerce. He accordingly applied himself with assiduity to the completion of his plan. The neighboring country being fertile, well settled, and abounding in grain, Mr. Stevenson contracted for considerable quantities of wheat; he freighted vessels and consigned them to a correspondent in his native country; the cargoes sold to great advantage, and returns were made equally beneficial. The commencement of a trade so lucrative to the first adventurers soon became an object of universal attention. Persons of a commercial and enterprising spirit emigrated from all quarters to this new and promising scene of industry. Wharfs were constructed; elegant and convenient habitations were rapidly erected; marshes were drained; spacious fields were occupied for the purposes of general utility; and within forty years from its first commencement Baltimore became not only the most wealthy and populous town in the province, but inferior to few on this continent, either in size, number of inhabitants, or the advantages arising from a well conducted and universal commercial connexion.*

The third place of importance in the province of Maryland is situated about seventy miles west of Annapolis, and is the capital of a most extensive, fertile, and populous county. Frederick Town is the name of this settlement. Within fifty years the river Monocacy, about three miles to the eastward, was the extreme boundary of cultivated establishments; and

* Soon after the appointment of Mr. Eden to the government of Maryland, Sir William Draper arrived in that province, on a tour throughout the continent. He contemplated the origin of Baltimore, and its rapid progress, with astonishment; and when introduced by the governor to the worthy founder, he elegantly accosted him by the appellation of the American Romulus.

Mr. D[ulany],[1] father to the present secretary of the province, was much censured for having procured considerable tracts of lands in the vicinity of that river, which it was generally supposed could not even repay the trifling charge of the purchase for many succeeding generations. The richness of the soil and the salubrity of the air operated, however, very powerfully to promote population; but what chiefly tended to the advancement of settlements in this remote district was the arrival of many emigrants from the Palatinate and other Germanic states. These people who, from their earliest days, had been disciplined in habits of industry, sobriety, frugality, and patience were peculiarly fitted for the laborious occupations of felling timber, clearing land, and forming the first improvements; and the success which attended their efforts induced multitudes of their enterprising countrymen to abandon their native homes to enjoy the plenteous harvest which appeared to await their labors in the wild, uncultivated wastes of America.

The Germans were not the only people sensible of the advantages to be derived from establishments in this interior country. Many British adventurers and natives of the coast, where land was becoming scarce and difficult to be acquired, were equally emulous on this occasion; and it is astonishing how soon extensive forests became highly cultivated, and promising settlements began on all sides to extend themselves.

To supply the real and imaginary necessities of those by whose persevering efforts and penetrating genius immense uncultivated tracts became flourishing establishments, storekeepers of various denominations were encouraged to pursue the path which industry had pointed out. Warehouses were accordingly erected, and woolens, linens, and

[1] Daniel Dulany the elder (1685-1753), sometime attorney general, commissary general, judge in vice-admiralty, and member of the council.

implements of husbandry were first presented to the view of the laborious planter. As wealth and population increased, wants were created, and many considerable demands, in consequence, took place for the various elegancies as well as necessaries of life; and thus, by imperceptible degrees, from an humble beginning, has Frederick Town arisen to its present flourishing state.

This place exceeds Annapolis in size and in the number of inhabitants. It contains one large and convenient church for the members of the established religion, and several chapels for the accommodation of the German and other dissenters. The buildings, though mostly of wood, have a neat and regular appearance. Provisions are cheap, plentiful, and excellent. In a word, here are to be found all conveniences and many superfluities; a lucrative trade is supported with the back country, and a considerable quantity of grain is sent from hence by land carriage to Baltimore for exportation to the European markets.

The above excepted, there are not any towns of consequence in the province of Maryland; the rest which bear that denomination are rather inconsiderable villages, the residence of a few merchants and storekeepers with a sufficient assortment of goods for the supply of the neighborhood.

Shipbuilding throughout this continent is a very lucrative and extensive branch of business; and I am assured by many, who are esteemed competent judges, that American vessels are, in general, molded in a very elegant and superior style. The immense quantity of useful timber to be found, even on the banks of almost every river, gives the shipwright peculiar advantages. These vessels, when perfectly completed, exclusive of particular decorations, are freighted with produce to some British port, and are generally sold after the delivery of their respective cargoes.

As an Englishman, I cannot but enjoy the reflection that

Great Britain will ever maintain a decided superiority in the durability and intrinsic value of her shipping. Were a judgment, indeed, to be formed from external appearances, a casual observer would not fail to decide, as to this article, in favor of Maryland and the adjacent provinces, American oak greatly exceeding the British in size and foliage; but when the growth is taken into consideration, a manifest advantage is evident in favor of the oaks of Britain. On this continent, this very useful and valuable timber attains its highest state of perfection in about fifty or sixty years; the natural consequence is, that being of a light and porous quality, it will not endure the depredations of time in any degree equal to that which advances by slow degrees to maturity. I have heard it asserted by persons of undoubted knowledge and experience that an English ship formed of solid and well-seasoned materials is worth more after a service of twenty years than the generality of American vessels that have sailed only seven.

This reason, I think, strongly operates against those who, penetrating into futurity, predict that the colonists must inevitably, before many years are passed, become great and formidable as a maritime power, since the necessity under which they must labor of frequently rebuilding in order to support a navy cannot but be attended with expenses that will require immense revenues, so as always to check their progress towards that distinction to which they may possibly aspire

LETTER VIII

In this remote region, my dear friend, the phantom pleasure is pursued with as much avidity as on your side of the Atlantic, and certainly with as much gratification, except by the injudicious herd who form ideas of happiness from comparison alone.

Our races, which are just concluded, continued four days, and afforded excellent amusement to those who are attached to the pleasures of the turf; and, surprising as it may appear, I assure you there are few meetings in England better attended, or where more capital horses are exhibited.

In order to encourage the breed of this noble animal, a jockey club has been instituted, consisting of many principal gentlemen in this and in the adjacent provinces, many of whom have imported from Britain, at a very great expense, horses of high reputation.

In America, the mild beauties of the autumnal months amply compensate for the fervent heats of summer and the rigid severity of winter. Nothing could exceed the charming serenity of the weather during these races, in consequence of which there was a prodigious concourse of spectators and considerable sums were depending on the contest of each day. On the first, a purse of one hundred guineas was run for, free only for the members of the club; and on the three following days subscription purses of fifty pounds each. Assemblies and theatrical representations were the amusements of the evening, at which the company exhibited a fashionable and brilliant appearance.

Our new theatre, of which I gave you an account in a former letter, was opened to a numerous audience the week preceding the races. The structure is not inelegant, but in my opinion on too narrow a scale for its length; the boxes are commodious and neatly decorated; the pit and gallery are calculated to hold a number of people without incommoding each other; the stage is well adapted for dramatic and pantomimical exhibitions; and several of the scenes reflect great credit on the ability of the painter. I have before observed that the performers are considerably above mediocrity; therefore little doubt can be entertained of their preserving the public favor and reaping a plenteous harvest.

Thus far on the article of pleasure. I shall conclude with an observation of a serious nature.

In the course of my excursions, I have conversed with divers intelligent planters, who emigrated to this country on account of various discouraging circumstances which baffled their utmost industry at home. A principal cause which has been assigned by very many for becoming adventurers in this part of the world is the custom, which is becoming too prevalent in England, of forming extensive farms for the accommodation of wealthy tenants and for greater facility in collecting the rents.

Whatever present advantages may arise from this practice, be assured a perseverance therein will be attended with consequences very prejudicial, for by this means a sensible depopulation will ensue; a considerable tract of country will be occupied by few inhabitants, and a multitude of valuable members of the community will be obliged to abandon their homes and connections and to court fortune in a distant region, where land may be procured for a trifling consideration and where the greatest encouragement is held out to skill and application.

Reason and experience incontestably prove that in the number of inhabitants consists the power and prosperity of the state. Agriculture, manufactures, and arts are founded on population, and a government naturally becomes wealthy and formidable by the strenuous exertions of industrious competition.

LETTER IX

Annapolis, December 24, 1771

The intense heat which prevails during the summer and the extremity of cold in winter I well know has been asserted to be highly prejudicial to the constitution; though for my own part I have not been sensible of any material inconvenience from the opposite quality of the seasons but have continued to enjoy uninterrupted health and spirits.

The variations of the weather are certainly more sudden in this part of America than even in the changeable climate of Britain. During one part of the day I have frequently thought the lightest apparel scarcely supportable, when in a moment a northwest wind has created sensations of a very different nature and a substantial suit of broadcloth has scarcely been sufficient to repel the cold.

Whatever you have heard relative to the rigid puritanical principles and economical habits of our American brethren is by no means true when applied to the inhabitants of the southern provinces. Liberality of sentiment and genuine hospitality are everywhere prevalent; and I am persuaded they too frequently mistake profuseness for generosity, and impair their health and their fortunes by splendor of appearance and magnificence of entertainments.

The quick importation of fashions from the mother country is really astonishing. I am almost inclined to believe that a new fashion is adopted earlier by the polished and affluent American than by many opulent persons in the great metropolis; nor are opportunities wanting to display superior elegance. We have varied amusements and numerous parties which afford to the young, the gay, and the ambitious an extensive field to contend in the race of vain and idle competition. In short, very little difference is, in reality, observable in the manners of the wealthy colonist and the wealthy Briton. Good and bad habits prevail on both sides the Atlantic.

It is but justice to confess that the American ladies possess a natural ease and elegance in the whole of their deportment; and that while they assiduously cultivate external accomplishments, they are still anxiously attentive to the more important embellishments of the mind. In conversation they are generally animated and entertaining, and deliver their sentiments with affability and propriety. In a word, there are, throughout these colonies, very many lovely women who have never passed the bounds of their respective provinces and yet, I am persuaded, might appear to great advantage in the most brilliant circles of gaiety and fashion.

In this country the marriage ceremony is universally performed in the dwelling houses of the parties. The company who are invited assemble early in the evening, and after partaking of tea and other refreshments, the indissoluble contract is completed. The bride and bridegroom then receive the accustomed congratulations; cards and dancing immediately succeed; an elegant supper, a cheerful glass, and the convivial song close the entertainment.

There are few places where young people are more frequently gratified with opportunities of associating together than in this country. Besides our regular assemblies, every mark of attention is paid to the patron saint of each parent dominion; and St. George, St. Andrew, St. Patrick, and St. David are celebrated with every partial mark of national attachment. General invitations are given, and the appearance is always numerous and splendid.

The Americans on this part of the continent have likewise a saint whose history, like those of the above venerable characters, is lost in fable and uncertainty. The first of May is, however, set apart to the memory of Saint Tamina, on which occasion the natives wear a piece of a buck's tail in their hats or in some conspicuous situation. During the course of the evening, and generally in the midst of a dance, the company are interrupted by the sudden intrusion of a number of persons habited like Indians, who rush violently into the room singing the war song, giving the whoop, and dancing in the style of those people, after which ceremony a collection is made and they retire well satisfied with their reception and entertainment.

In this province there are scarce any vestiges of the original inhabitants, but it does not appear that their numbers have been reduced by any inhuman or indirect practices of the British settlers. In Dorset County[1] on the eastern shore of Maryland, there are indeed the remains of a nation, once populous and powerful, who to this day retain considerable tracts of valuable land for which they receive an annual consideration but by no means equivalent to the real value. When every other Indian nation thought it necessary to retire beyond the range of the European settlements, these people it seems determined to continue on their native spot. But being precluded from their former occupations and pursuits, they became totally indolent and inactive; and a different habit of living, a violent propensity to spirituous liquors, and the havoc occasioned by the smallpox and other disorders, to which they were unaccustomed, reduced their numbers to such a degree that at this time not twenty of their descendants remain.

Since no charge of cruelty can justly be adduced, it becomes a natural enquiry what is become of those numerous tribes that formerly occupied this fertile territory?

---

[1] Dorchester County was frequently called Dorset even in the official records before the Revolution.

Maryland, comparatively, is a small province, bounded on the west by the interior counties of Virginia and Pennsylvania; the Indians, from their particular mode of living, require an extensive circuit, depending principally on hunting for their support; and wherever their game becomes scarce, they instantly quit that country for a more eligible situation. As this colony became populous by the arrival and natural increase of the new adventurers, the aborigines were circumscribed in their ancient limits and were consequently induced to relinquish their possessions, for a supposed equivalent, and retire to a more extensive field of action.

From what cause I cannot ascertain, but the North American Indians have never yet been known to incorporate with Europeans; nor has any progress yet been made in civilizing their manners or in reclaiming them from that ignorance in which they are universally involved. Their habits appear rooted beyond the possibility of conviction to remove; the present moment engrosses every thought, regardless of the events of futurity.

LETTER X

It is true, my friend, that America is rapidly increasing in population and importance: but a continent so extensive must be very thinly inhabited for many generations. Agriculture must, therefore, be the grand object of colonial attention to a very distant period. While the people can be more profitably employed, as they now are, in clearing and cultivating land, it will be their interest to import the various manufactures of the mother country, it being evident that every species of goods may be obtained much cheaper, and of a superior quality, through the medium of commercial intercourse, than by any patriotic exertions amongst themselves.

Throughout the whole of the American provinces there are immense tracts of unappropriated lands. In every government, offices are established under regal or proprietary authority for the purpose of granting the same to adventurers on stipulated terms. As the method of proceeding in this business is nearly similar in every part of the continent, an account of the mode adopted with us will give you a general idea of this matter. Take, therefore, the following detail, which I have transcribed from an official record, for your information.

All papers relating to the granting of vacant land within this province issue out and are recorded in the land office; and the mode pursued to effect the grant of such vacant lands is by warrants, either special or common. If the lands are cultivated or improved, they cannot be effected by any other than a special warrant, specifying the particular location and quantity to be effected. And all such warrants issue in consequence of an order from the proprietary's agent, intimating that the caution money of five pounds sterling *per* hundred acres is paid. The warrant is directed to the surveyor of the county where the land lies, who makes a survey and returns a certificate thereof into the land office, from whence it is transmitted to the examiner general, and after examination it is again sent back to the land office: a patent, or grant, then issues on the certificate, subject to the payment of an annual rent of four shillings sterling for every hundred acres. The fees attending granting the warrant, of the survey in consequence, of the examination of the certificate, issuing patent thereon, and affixing the great seal of the province thereto, will amount to about the sum of seven or eight pounds currency *per* hundred acres.

The same mode is exactly pursued in common warrants to effect uncultivated lands, but the expenses are rather less.

It is to be observed the aforesaid warrants are to effect lands never before taken up. There are other warrants that issue out of the land office, such as warrants of resurvey, escheat warrants, and warrants under the proclamation.

The first of these are granted to resurvey a tract of land already patented, and in which the petitioner has a fee simple; and to add all or any contiguous vacancy, whether cultivated or otherwise. This warrant, as well as all others, must be executed or renewed within the first six months from the time of granting, otherwise they are of no force or effect; and any vacant land added, if not paid for within two years from the date of the warrant (agreeable to sundry proclamations published), will become subject and liable to the benefit of the first discoverer thereof. And hence the proclamation warrants take their rise, *for they and no other warrants* can legally effect lands thus circumstanced.

Warrants of escheat are only granted in instances where the original patentees, or persons claiming under them, have died seised in fee, intestate, and without heirs, of tracts of land heretofore granted, with liberty given of effecting as well such original tracts of escheat as any vacant land thereto adjoining. The composition money payable as in the above cases; with this distinction, that the quality of the escheat land, and improvements thereon, are more particularly described by the surveyor, and from such description the agent, or receiver-general, ascertains the real value of the land so escheated. The petitioner is entitled to one third of the full valuation of the escheat for the discovery; and the residue, together with any vacancy added, must be paid for to entitle him to a grant. The fees and expenses incidental to all these warrants are considerably more than in primitive surveys, and cannot be particularly ascertained till the whole business is completed.

By an instruction from the Board of Revenue, no certificate whatever can be patented, though every requisite be complied with, till it has lain three months in the office. The intention of this instruction is to give persons who might be injured by the operation of secret surveys an opportunity of contesting such surveys by a caveat.

The land office, and all offices respecting the proprietary's revenue, are, in a great measure, subject to the control of the board of revenue, which was established by the late Lord Proprietary. Upon a declaration of a caveat in the land office, if it should be dissatisfactory to the parties, they may appeal to the board of revenue, and have the matter reheard and determined by them.

The annual revenue of the proprietary arising from the sale of lands and the yearly quit rent, after deducting all the various charges of government, averages at twelve thousand five hundred pounds *per annum*. All offices excepting those in the service of the customs are in his gift, or in the gift of his representative for the time being. This patronage includes a very extensive range of lucrative and respectable stations, and consequently throws great weight and influence into the scale of government.

This influence is considered by many as inimical to the essential interests of the people; a spirit of party is consequently excited, and every idea of encroachment is resisted by the popular faction with all the warmth of patriotic enthusiasm.

I have before observed that elections in this province are triennial. The delegates returned are generally persons of the greatest consequence in their different counties; and many of them are perfectly acquainted with the political and commercial interests of their constituents. I have frequently heard subjects debated with great powers of eloquence and force of reason; and the utmost regularity and propriety distinguish the whole of their proceedings.

During the sitting of the assembly the members of both houses receive a stated sum for their attendance on public business; and the number of days being properly certified, they are regularly paid their respective claims at the conclusion of each session.*

Provincial and county magistrates are appointed by the governor. The former are commissioned to try capital offenses and important causes relative to property; the latter preside in the county courts. They have likewise, individually, power to determine causes of the value of forty shillings and to inflict punishment on servants, complaint being regularly made and the matter proved by their employers.

The governor has a discretionary authority to pardon persons capitally convicted; and by the principles of the constitution he is obliged to sign all warrants for the execution of those who suffer agreeable to sentence.

A litigious spirit is very apparent in this country. The assizes are held twice in the year in the city of Annapolis, and the number of causes then brought forward is really incredible. Though few of the gentlemen who practice in the courts have been regularly called to the bar, there are several who are confessedly eminent in their profession; and those who are possessed of superior abilities have full employ-

---

* Members of the upper house, nine shillings sterling *per diem;* those of the lower, about eight shillings and sixpence.

ment for the exertion of their talents, and are paid in due proportion by their respective clients.

The natives of these provinces, even those who move in the humbler circles of life, discover a shrewdness and penetration not generally observable in the mother country. On many occasions they are inquisitive even beyond the bounds of propriety; they discriminate characters with the greatest accuracy, and there are few who do not seem perfectly conversant with the general and particular interests of the community. An idea of equality also seems generally to prevail, and the inferior order of people pay but little external respect to those who occupy superior stations.

LETTER XI

Annapolis, September 7, 1772

I am just returned from an excursion to the frontiers of this province, in which my curiosity was highly gratified. It is impossible to conceive a more rich and fertile country than I have lately traversed; and when it becomes populous in proportion to its extent, Frederick County will at least be equal to the most desirable establishment on this side the Atlantic.

In the back settlements, where the inhabitants are but thinly scattered, the face of the country even at this luxuriant season of the year exhibited in many places a dreary appearance. Lands to a very considerable extent are taken up by persons who, looking to futurity for greater advantages, are content to clear gradually some portions of their domains for immediate subsistence. Not having the means to fell and carry their timber away, they make a deep incision with an axe entirely round each trunk, at the distance of about four feet from the ground, which occasions the leaves almost instantly to wither; and before the total decay of the tree, Indian corn may be cultivated to great advantage amidst the immense trunks that fill the dreary forest.

To have the idea of winter impressed on the mind from external appearances at a time when nature is fainting beneath the intense heat of an autumnal sun, is, I am inclined to believe, peculiar to this country. In some districts, far as the eye could extend the leafless trees of an astonishing magnitude crowded on the sight, the creeping ivy only

66

denoting vegetation; at the same time, the face of the earth was covered with golden crops, which promised

Richly to repay the anxious toil.

The habitations of the planters in this remote district of the province are, in general, of a rude construction, the timber with which they frame their dwellings seldom undergoing the operation of any tool except the axe. An apartment to sleep in and another for domestic purposes, with a contiguous storehouse and conveniences for their livestock, at present gratify their utmost ambition. Their method of living perfectly corresponds with their exterior appearance. Indian corn, beaten in a mortar and afterwards baked or boiled, forms a dish which is the principal subsistence of the indigent planter and is even much liked by many persons of a superior class. This, when properly prepared, is called *hominy*, and when salt beef, pork, or bacon is added, no complaints are made respecting their fare.

Throughout the whole of this province, fruit is not only plentiful but excellent in various kinds. There are very few plantations unprovided with an apple and a peach orchard; the peach trees are all standards, and without the assistance of art frequently produce fruit of an exquisite flavor.

In the woods, I have often met with vines twining round trees of different denominations, and have gathered from them bunches of grapes of a tolerable size and not unpleasant to the palate. In process of time, when the colonists are enabled to pay attention to their natural advantages, they will, assuredly, possess all the superfluities as well as the conveniences of life without the necessity of recurring to foreign assistance. Even sugar, of a tolerable quality, they will be able to manufacture without application to the British islands. A planter at whose house I partook of some refreshment produced a quantity of that capital luxury, the grain of which was tolerable and the taste not disagreeable. This, he assured me, was the produce of his own possessions, extracted by incision from a tree, great numbers of which grow throughout the interior regions of the American provinces.* The simple process of boiling brought the luscious liquid to a proper consistency; and he was persuaded, whenever more important concerns would permit a necessary attention to this article, the inhabitants of the British colonies would be amply supplied from their own inexhaustible resources.

About thirty miles west of Frederick Town I passed through a settlement which is making quick advances to perfection. A German adventurer, whose name is Hagar,[1] purchased a considerable tract of land in this neighborhood, and with much discernment and foresight determined to give encouragement to traders and to erect proper habitations for the stowage of goods for the supply of the adjacent country. His plan succeeded; he has lived to behold a multitude of inhabitants on lands which he remembered unoccupied; and he has seen erected in places, appropriated by him for that purpose, more than an hundred comfortable edifices, to which the name of Hagerstown is given in honor of the intelligent founder.

* The maple tree.

[1] Jonathan Hagar (1714-1775) laid out Hagerstown in 1762. Of German extraction (naturalized 1747), he was by British law not eligible to sit in the provincial assembly. When elected as delegate from Frederick County the assembly passed a special enabling act to seat him. Fluid eighteenth-century orthography gave the town he founded a spelling slightly different from the correct spelling of his name.

LETTER XII

LETTERS FROM AMERICA

Annapolis, October 3, 1772

By an act of the assembly of this province a residence of three years is requisite as a qualification for holding any office immediately dependent on the proprietary. This regulation affords security against the intrusion of strangers who might arrive from the mother country under a patronage too strong for any local interest.

Having happily completed the limited term, I have begun to experience the bounty of my patron, and find myself already in possession of an office of trust and respectability, and not unauthorized to look forward to a still better provision. I hope it is unnecessary to say that I am content and grateful under such circumstances, and yet there is something which seems to obscure my prospect and to lessen that happiness which would otherwise be complete.

It is I know both imprudent and culpable "to shape the fashion of uncertain evils"; yet it is almost impossible to avoid drawing unfavorable conclusions from that spirit of party which, at this time, appears predominant throughout the British colonies.

Under pretense of supporting the sacred claims of freedom and of justice factious and designing men are industriously fomenting jealousy and discontent; and unless they are stopped in their progress by the immediate and determined exertions of the wise and moderate, they will aggravate the dissension, which is become but too evident, and involve this now happy country in complicated misery.

You may remember that I have occasionally attempted to give my thoughts a poetical dress, and you have been pleased to favor my humble efforts with your partial indulgence. The following lines, the result of reflections on the political state of this empire, I was tempted to give to the editor of the *Maryland Gazette,*[1] in which they have appeared with some degree of approbation.

Blest was that age when, free from madening strife,
    The peaceful shepherd told his plaintive tale;
And, free from all those cares that harrass life,
    Found real bliss sequester'd in the vale.

Content alone, with ardor, he pursu'd,
    He trac'd her footsteps in the shady grove;
His fleecy wealth around he joyous view'd,
    And sung, in artless strains, the force of love!

No proud aspiring thoughts perplex'd his breast,
    Or search of sordid gain his peace destroy'd;
Blithe was each day — and when he sunk to rest,
    Sweet were the slumbers which he then enjoy'd.

To polish life, fair Science rear'd her head,
    And numerous arts appear'd to deck the land;
Truths moral, and divine their influence shed,
    And social virtues clos'd the shining band.

O had mankind, with noblest views elate,
    Improv'd the blessings Heaven in bounty gave,
Then had they not suppos'd a partial fate,
    Or shrunk, with horror, from the gloomy grave.

Founded on rapine powerful empires rose,
    And wild Ambition rul'd the human mind,

---

[1] The *Maryland Gazette* was published at Annapolis in these years by Anna Catharine Green and her sons by her deceased husband Jonas Green. This effusion appeared in the issue dated July 23, 1772.

Fell Discord pour'd around her baleful woes,
　　And friends were faithless! — lovers were unkind!

The scepter'd tyrant, swoln with hopes of fame!
　　Exulting thunders from the gorgeous car!
Dooms realms to slaughter for a pompous name,
　　And proudly glories in the guilt of war!

By stern oppression struck, the helpless poor,
　　From much-lov'd cottages, and hamlets fly;
Depriv'd of all, from Heaven they aid implore,
　　Neglected droop, and unlamented die!

Religion! sent by Heaven to heal each grief,
　　To point the road where human evils cease;
Give rankling misery a sure relief;
　　And sooth the warring passions into peace;

By bigot Zeal, and Superstition fir'd,
　　With horrid Fury scatters death around;
And deems that wretch most pious, — most inspir'd,
　　Who strikes, with ruthless hand, the direful wound!

Sea-girt Britannia! mistress of the isles!
　　Where Faith, and Liberty, united reign;
Around whose fertile shores glad Nature smiles,
　　And Ceres crowns with gifts the industrious swain!

Thy generous daring sons have nobly toil'd,
　　To guard thy cliffs from arbitrary sway;
In well fought fields the baffled tyrant foil'd,
　　Where glorious Freedom led the arduous way!

Now through the land Dissention stalks confest;
　　With foul Distrust, and Hatred in her train;
The dire infection runs from breast to breast,
　　And statesmen plan — and patriots plead in vain!

All-gracious Heaven, avert the impending storm,
  Bid every jealous, jarring faction cease;
Let sweet Content resume her lovely form,
  And o'er the land diffuse perpetual peace:

And, when again our colours are unfurl'd,
  May Britons nobly join one common cause!
With rapid conquests strike the wondering world,
  In firm support of Liberty and Laws.

LETTER XIII

Annapolis, February 20, 1773

Your observations on the resources of America are well founded. I grant they are infinite, and I am persuaded that in process of time she will be enabled to avail herself of innumerable advantages; but those that assert she will effectually rival Great Britain in that invaluable staple of her commerce, the *woolen manufactory,* are indeed by far too sanguine in their expectation; coarse cloths for the wear of servants and negroes the colonists may probably be enabled to manufacture, but insurmountable objections arise to the production of those of a superior quality.

To judge of this climate by the parallel degrees of latitude in Europe, it is natural to conclude that the middle provinces experience very little of the rigor of winter, and that in fact their greatest inconvenience must arise from intense heat during the summer months. But extraordinary as it may appear, this country, from local circumstances, is accustomed to every severity of the opposite seasons. I assure you that I have been less sensible of the influence of the sun in the hottest seasons in the island of Jamaica than in this part of British America; and I am credibly informed that no material difference prevails from New York inclusive to the southern extremity of Virginia. To the northward of New York the winters continue longer, the cold is equally intense, and the summer for its short duration hot in proportion. South of Virginia the climate gradually becomes similar to the torrid zone; consequently the wool degenerates, in a regular proportion, until the external covering of the sheep becomes at last a strong coarse hair resembling that of goats.

In Maryland and in the adjacent provinces the cold is more severe from January till the beginning of May than in any part of the island of Great Britain, in consequence of which the American farmer is reduced to the necessity of housing his sheep during that rigid season. Summer may literally be said to be seated on the lap of winter, and the immediate transition from cold to heat is evidently extremely prejudicial to the growth and improvement of wool, so that in quality it is greatly inferior; nor is the quantity produced proportionable to what is yielded in the milder regions of the parent state.

Under these disadvantages it may reasonably be concluded that the American settlements will ever be necessitated to look up to Britain for a very considerable supply of her invaluable staple. And even if these causes did not operate, many years must unavoidably elapse before the colonists can establish or conduct manufactures in such a manner as to enable them to supply even their own wants on terms of greater advantage than by relying on external assistance.

This immense continent will require a considerable population before the inhabitants can with any propriety divert their attention from agriculture. To settle and to cultivate lands must be their first great object; and the produce of those exertions they must barter in exchange for European manufactures. In vain is encouragement held forth to induce ingenious artisans to emigrate from their original situations. On their arrival either the allurements which tempted them deceive their expectations, or the natural wish to obtain a permanent establishment supersedes every other consideration, and induces a great majority of these adventurers to purchase lands which comparatively bear no price, and the purchasers are reduced to rely on time and industry to recompence their assiduity.

Another circumstance, very important in its nature, likewise demands attention. The price of labor must be greatly lessened before the Americans can possibly manufacture to any advantage; and this inconvenience cannot be remedied until by an overplus of people there are competitors in every art, and a sufficient number of opulent inhabitants to encourage and reward their ingenuity.

At present, it is evident that almost every article of use or ornament is to be obtained on much more reasonable terms from the mother country than from artisans settled on this side the Atlantic. It is also as certain that goods of every kind produced or manufactured in England are greatly superior to the produce or manufactures of this continent. In process of time, but a time far distant, the colonies may, undoubtedly, from their great resources, be enabled to rival Britain in many valuable articles of commerce. But in your grand staple, the growth and manufacture of wool, you will, in a general point of view, stand *single* and *preeminent*. Nature in this particular has been exuberantly bountiful. Your fertile downs are a source of inexhaustible wealth. Support that superiority, which the benevolence of heaven has blessed you with, by a judicious and industrious exertion of local advantages, and the power and splendor of Great Britain will defy the utmost efforts of opposition and remain for ages with undiminished luster!

LETTER XIV

Annapolis, October 4, 1773

I thank you, my dear friend, for your very entertaining and very descriptive detail of the extensive improvements now carrying forward in the British metropolis. If I may presume to compare small things with great, even here we are making considerable advances towards perfection.

About the close of the year 1769, an act of assembly was passed to erect a new State House on a very enlarged and beautiful plan.[1] This work has been carried on with great dispatch, and when completed will at least be equal to any public edifice on the American continent. The legislature of this province, animated by sentiments which reflect the highest credit on their patriotism and wisdom, have also determined by a recent law to endow and found a college for the education of youth in every liberal and useful branch of science. An institution of this nature was most strongly recommended to their consideration by our worthy governor at an early period after his arrival in this country; and to his laudable and persevering exertions the public are materially indebted for the establishment of a seminary which, as it will be conducted under excellent regulations, will shortly preclude the necessity of crossing the Atlantic for the completion of a classical and polite education.

---

[1] The reference here is to the third State House, which is still in use. Morris L. Radoff, *Buildings of the State of Maryland at Annapolis* (Publication No. 9, Hall of Records Commission, Annapolis, 1954).

During the administration of Mr. B[laden],[2] who presided over this province from the year 1742 to the year 1747, a noble mansion was projected for the residence of the governor of Maryland. A delightful situation was appropriated for this purpose on the banks of the Severn, within the limits of the city of Annapolis, commanding in every point of view the most interesting and beautiful objects. Materials of every kind were provided equal to the spirit of public liberality, and the building was nearly completed in a style of superior magnificence when an unhappy contention took place between the governor and the delegates of the people which increased to such a degree that, at a period when a very trifling sum would have rendered it a noble habitation, the further prosecution of the design was discontinued, and it has remained to this day a melancholy and moldering monument of the consequences resulting from political dissensions.[3] The depredations of time have very greatly injured the interior parts of this edifice, which in an unfinished state has continued many years exposed to every inclemency of weather. However, on a late accurate survey, the outside structure and the principal timbers are found in a condition so perfect that it is determined to repair the damages sustained, and to apply the building to the purposes of collegiate education, for which every circumstance contributes to render it truly eligible. The adjacent country is open and healthy; the contiguous grounds are sufficiently extensive for the advantages of exercise and amusement; and the fabric

[2] Thomas Bladen (1698-1780), governor of Maryland 1742-1747 and later member of parliament from the rotten borough of Old Sarum. Bladen married Barbara Janssen, sister of Lady Baltimore.

[3] This unfinished structure was dubbed "Bladen's Folly" by the townspeople of Annapolis. The legislature toyed several times with the idea of completing the building for a college but the proposal Eddis mentions came to nothing. After the Revolution the rebuilding finally came about. Today this structure, under the name McDowell Hall, is the administration building of St. John's College.

will contain a variety of spacious and commodious apartments for the accommodation of the professors and students.

Institutions of this nature are inseparably connected with the interest and happiness of these provinces; but with respect to the parent state they may possibly be attended with serious consequences. When the real or supposed necessity ceases of sending the youth of this continent to distant seminaries for the completion of their education, the attachment of the colonies to Great Britain will gradually weaken, and a less frequent intercourse will tend to encourage those sentiments of self importance which have already taken too deep root and which, I fear, the utmost exertions of political wisdom will never be able wholly to eradicate. As an Englishman I therefore cannot but view with a partial regret every adopted plan that may possibly, in the event, lessen or alienate the affection of the colonists. And though I am sensible the good of the whole ought to supersede every private consideration, yet I cannot anticipate the future importance and prosperity of America without a most fervent prayer that every advantage she may derive from her exertions may ultimately depend on a permanent and constitutional connection with the mother country.

To the number of public erections a new church is likewise to be added, the design of which does great credit to the genius of the architect.[4] It will be large, neat, and commodious; and is to be built on the site of the ancient edifice, from which many materials will be furnished. This work is to be executed as soon as possible; and we may reasonably expect, if these different undertakings are conducted with judgment and spirit, that they will be considered as valuable monuments of that refined taste which so remarkably characterizes the present times.

[4] The sanctuary in which Eddis attended services was the first St. Anne's Church, illustrated in Radoff, *Buildings of the State of Maryland*, Plate 6. The plan for a new church fell victim to the revolutionary troubles; the church was not consecrated until 1792.

LETTER XV

Annapolis, November 8, 1773

"As water to a thirsty soul, so is news from a far country."
Your circumstantial letter of the fourteenth of September
afforded me the greatest satisfaction. I was at once entertained and instructed by your very judicious and pointed
observations on the present political system. The repeal of
the Stamp Act was a wise and necessary measure; but on
what principle subsequent laws have been enacted, which
have evidently the like tendency, I am at a loss to determine.
Were the duties to be regularly collected in consequence of
the acts now in force, the revenue arising from them would
really be inconsiderable. Nor do the colonists ground their
objections on the sums which, by this means, would be levied on the importation of the enumerated articles; but they
assert that the principle on which they resist the operation of
these laws is briefly this: "That they are wholly unconstitutional; and that to admit their legality in a single instance
would undoubtedly be to admit a right which might be considered by the legislature of Great Britain as a sufficient authority to tax them at some future period in any proportion
adequate to the real or supposed exigencies of the state."
How far they are to be justified in this opinion I am not
competent to determine; but it is evident that on this side
the Atlantic a spirit of discontent universally prevails; and
there are many desponding individuals here and in other
provinces who already pretend to penetrate so deep into the

events of futurity as to foretell the most serious consequences.

From trivial cause, what mighty evils spring!

For my part, I will not indulge apprehensions of so melancholy a nature.

I have lately received a very sensible and very entertaining letter from my valued correspondent, Miss M[artha More], who informs me that her sister H[annah][1] has, at length, complied with the requisition of many judicious and impartial friends and has ventured into public notice, in defiance of criticism. On the 10th of May last, her pastoral poem, *The Search After Happiness,* made its first appearance; and so rapid has been its success that a second large impression took place early in August.[2] Lord Lyttelton,[3] whose refined taste and accurate discernment is universally acknowledged, has honored the amiable author with a letter expressive of his warmest approbation; and the public prints are unanimous in bearing testimony to her merit. The copy I have received is in continual circulation, and indeed, it must argue a vitiated and depraved judgment in the reader not to be charmed with a production formed on a plan subservient to the great interests of religion and virtue, and decorated with all the graces and embellishments of poetry.

After paying this just tribute to the talents of a lady who,

[1] Hannah More (1745-1833) earned from Dr. Johnson the dubious description, "the most powerful versificatrix in the English language." She produced twenty-four volumes of poetry and prose during her lifetime. Her sister Martha (d. 1819) was Eddis' correspondent.

[2] *The Search After Happiness,* a pastoral drama designed for school children to learn by heart instead of less edifying works, went through eleven editions by 1796.

[3] George Lyttelton (1709-1773), first Baron Lyttelton, patron of literature and minor author of prose and verse. Eddis' regard was not shared by Smollett, Chesterfield, and Dr. Johnson, who lampooned Lyttelton's pretensions.

I trust, will soon attain a distinguished rank in the literary world, I shall venture to conclude this letter by the insertion of an epilogue, which I wrote a few months since at the request of a friend for the benefit of a comedian at the theater in Philadelphia. As I am informed it was received with approbation by a numerous audience, I shall venture with the greater confidence to add this little poetical effusion to your manuscript collection.

OCCASIONAL EPILOGUE

When stern Oppression rear'd her baleful head,
To this blest clime our free-born fathers fled:
Secure from lawless sway, they chearful toil'd,
And soon the grateful glebe with plenty smil'd;
Cities arose, while Commerce pour'd her store,
And wealth flow'd in from every distant shore.
Now polish'd ease, and manners shine confest,
While ardent Freedom warms each generous breast:
Dark brooding Ignorance has wing'd her flight,
And heav'n-born Science beams with radiant light:
The sister arts, with rapid progress rise;
Proud lofty towers and columns reach the skies:
The genial virtues here united reign,
And modest Merit never sues in vain.
Among the numerous objects of your care,
Let this, our moral stage, your goodness share:
Fir'd with your praise, dependant still on you,
The steep ascent with ardor we pursue;
No ribald scenes we offer to your sight,
But "such as Virtue views with fond delight."
Bold is the attempt, in various forms to please,
And, Proteus-like, shift every form with ease;
In quick transition ever yet to move,
From comic humour, to disastrous love!
Trace Nature's paths, nor deviate from her laws,
Which can alone secure a just applause.
I, who am yet a novice on the stage,

What claim have I, your favour to engage?
Yet, spite of each defect, still have I found,
Beyond my fondest hopes, my wishes crown'd.
O still assist me, while I boldly aim
To catch some portion of dramatic fame:
So may kind Heaven repay your generous aid,
And rankling sorrows ne'er your peace invade;
But, bless'd supremely, may you ever prove
The sweets of Liberty! — the joys of Love!

LETTER XVI

Annapolis, January 3, 1774

The American prints will inform you, ere you receive this, of the recent proceedings at Boston. The whole quantity of tea contained on board three vessels, amounting to three hundred and forty-two chests, was on the 16th of December immersed in the bay. The East India Company are the only sufferers on this occasion, as all accounts perfectly correspond in asserting that this hasty business was transacted without the least detriment to private property. New York, Philadelphia, Charleston, and other places it is universally imagined will pursue similar measures. Vast as this continent is, the inhabitants appear animated to a degree of frenzy with the same spirit of opposition. Where the consequences will terminate Heaven knows! If a judgment may be formed from the present disposition of the people, I will venture to assert that not the least future taxation will ever be admitted here without what they conceive a legal representation.

As an Englishman warmly attached to my native country and anxious for its honor and prosperity, I view the impending storm with inexpressible inquietude. I fear, my friend, our statesmen have promoted measures which they will be equally embarrassed to enforce or defend. But these are matters too high for my discussion; I detest politics, and shall, therefore, leave you to make your own comments. I and mine are well; would I could say we were perfectly happy! Have I not reason to apprehend my establishment is not so permanent as my flattering ideas had suggested? Should the storm burst, it must inevitably involve in the same ruin multitudes who think differently and are equally actuated by conscientious principles

LETTER XVII

All America is in a flame! I hear strange language every
day. The colonists are ripe for any measures that will tend
to the preservation of what they call their natural liberty. I
enclose you the resolves of *our* citizens; *they* have caught the
general contagion.* Expresses are flying from province to

---

* At a meeting of the inhabitants of the city of Annapolis on Wednesday,
the twenty-fifth day of May, 1774, after notice given of the time, place, and
occasion of this meeting:

Resolved, that it is the unanimous opinion of this meeting, that the
town of Boston is now suffering in the common cause of America, and
that it is incumbent on every colony in America to unite in effectual
measures to obtain a repeal of the late act of Parliament for blocking up
the harbor of Boston.

That it is the opinion of this meeting, that if the colonies come into a
joint resolution to stop all importation from, and exportations to Great
Britain, till the said act be repealed, the same will preserve North America
and her liberties.

Resolved therefore, That the inhabitants of this city will join in an
association with the several counties of this province, and the principal
provinces of America, to put an immediate stop to all exports to Great
Britain, and that after a short day, hereafter to be agreed on, that there
shall be no imports from Great Britain, till the said act be repealed, and
that such association be on oath.

That it is the opinion of this meeting, that the gentlemen of the law of
this province bring no suit for the recovery of any debt due from any
inhabitant of this province to any inhabitant of Great Britain, until the said
act be repealed.

That the inhabitants of this city will, and it is the opinion of this meeting, that this province ought immediately to break off all trade and dealings

province. It is the universal opinion *here* that the mother country cannot support a contention with these settlements, if they abide steady to the letter and spirit of their associations. Where will these matters end? Imagination anticipates with horror the most dreadful consequences. If the measures adopted at home are founded on the principles of justice, it will become administration to be firm and decisive. If they are not, it will be advisable, even on the score of interest, not to abandon the substance for a shadow. True policy will suggest the expediency of embracing a conciliatory system.

June 5th

The governor left Annapolis on the twenty-eighth of last month, in order to embark for England, where his private concerns require for a time his presence. He is now with his friend, Colonel Fitzhugh, at the mouth of the Patuxent. His dispatches are to leave town this evening, as the ship will certainly sail in the course of the week.

You will observe that the enclosed resolutions of the citizens of Annapolis took place in consequence of the act of parliament for blocking up the harbor of Boston.

The meeting at which these resolutions were passed was on Wednesday the twenty-fifth of May. But as it was evident that the majority by which they were carried did not consist of the most respectable inhabitants, a protest made its appearance on the ensuing Monday signed by one hundred

---

with that colony or province which shall refuse or decline to come into similar resolutions with a majority of the colonies.

That Messieurs John Hall, Charles Carroll, Thomas Johnson, Jr., William Paca, Matthias Hammond, and Samuel Chase, be a committee for this city, to join with those who shall be appointed for Baltimore Town and other parts of this province to constitute one general committee; and that the gentlemen appointed for this city immediately correspond with Baltimore Town and other parts of this province to effect such association as will secure American liberty.

and thirty-five persons,* amongst whom are to be found many of the first importance in this city and in the neighborhood. You will, I doubt not, be pleased to see that I have taken this opportunity of avowing my sentiments on a subject which equally affects private reputation and public faith.

* TO THE PRINTERS

May 30, 1774

A publication of the enclosed protest, supported by the names of a considerable number of the inhabitants of the city of Annapolis, will, it is presumed, furnish the most authentic grounds for determining the sense of the majority on a question of the last importance.

We whose names are subscribed, inhabitants of the city of Annapolis, conceive it our clear right and most incumbent duty to express our cordial and explicit disapprobation of a resolution which was carried by forty-seven against thirty-one at the meeting held on the 27th instant.

The resolution against which we protest, in the face of the world, is the following.

"That it is the opinion of this meeting that the gentlemen of the law of this province bring no suit for the recovery of any debt due from any inhabitant of this province to any inhabitant of Great Britain until the said act be repealed." — *Dissentient.*

First, because we are impressed with a full conviction that this resolution is founded in treachery and rashness, inasmuch as it is big with bankruptcy and ruin to those inhabitants of Great Britain who, relying with unlimited security on our good faith and integrity, have made us masters of their fortunes; condemning them *unheard,* for not having interposed their influence with parliament in favor of the town of Boston, without duly weighing the force with which that influence would probably have operated; or whether in their conduct they were actuated by wisdom and policy, or by *corruption* and *avarice.*

Secondly, because whilst the inhabitants of Great Britain are partially despoiled of every legal remedy to recover what is justly due to them, no provision is made to prevent us from being harassed by the prosecution of internal suits, but our fortunes and persons are left at the mercy of domestic creditors, without a possibility of extricating ourselves, unless by a general convulsion, an event, in the contemplation of sober reason, replete with horror.

Thirdly, because our credit, as a commercial people, will expire under the wound; for what confidence can possibly be reposed in those who shall have exhibited the most avowed and most striking proof that they are not bound by obligations as sacred as human invention can suggest.

I need not mention that it is *a particular resolution* against which the protest is leveled, the others being of too popular a nature to admit of opposition. And, indeed, the generality of those who have ventured to assert the claims of honor to discharge their pecuniary obligations to the mother country are considered, by the more violent party, as actuated by sentiments inimical to the interests of America; and it is even said that they would combat every attempt to obtain a repeal of the obnoxious acts, if they were not apprehensive of incurring the just resentment of an injured people. For my own part, I verily believe that the majority of the subscribers are influenced by motives which reflect the highest credit on their integrity, independent of political considerations.

It is here necessary that I clear up a seeming contradiction. The resolutions inserted in the *Gazette* are dated the twenty-fifth: the protest alludes to transactions on the twenty-seventh. After the publication of the resolves entered into in consequence of the meeting held on the first mentioned day, several gentlemen of influence and respectability had the courage to declare, in the most express terms, that if the sentiments of the people were properly collected, it would not appear that the WHOLE of the proceedings received their unanimous approbation. To obviate this objection, handbills were distributed, and a general attendance was earnestly requested, in consequence of which, on the evening of the twenty-seventh, a second assembly of the citizens took place. But instead of associating with that ardor the zealous partisans expected, ONLY seventy-eight persons were mustered on the important occasion. Had the whole number of those whose principles were directed by moderation thought it safe or prudent to appear in support of their sentiments, the iniquitous resolution, against which we have protested, would not have publicly appeared to the discredit of our province; even admitting the conduct of government with respect to this continent to be founded on maxims subversive of the constitution. Surely, in a moral point of view, it is highly criminal to attempt, by unjust or indirect methods, to obtain a redress of the most oppressive grievances.

In these tempestuous times, your dear sister supports her spirits wonderfully; yet are there moments when she yields to boding apprehensions and anticipates the renewal of sorrows and disappointments. She has, however, this consolation to support her: that whatever sufferings may be our portion, we shall share them with each other.

It is my solemn determination, without regard to motives of interest or safety, to act strictly upon principle. And though *my* conduct will be of very little importance, considered in a *public* point of view, yet under all the varied circumstances of prosperity or distress, the reflection of having acted agreeably to the dictates of conscience will enhance the advantages of affluence or animate the mind to sustain, with becoming fortitude, the most painful and unmerited reverse of fortune.

That the general tranquility may be speedily reestablished is the fervent prayer of your faithful, etc.

LETTER XVIII

Annapolis, October 26, 1774

The general attention is fixed on the Congress now sitting in Philadelphia, and all descriptions of people are waiting for the result of their deliberations with the utmost impatience.

The Canada Bill is as unpopular here as the Boston Port Bill and adds greatly to the universal discontent. The provinces are unanimous in the cause of their northern brethren, and contribute largely in supplying their necessities. The spirit of opposition to ministerial measures appears to blaze steadily and equally in every part of British America, and unless some speedy alteration takes place in the political system the consequences must inevitably be dreadful.

Every well-wisher to the interest and happiness of the mother country and her colonies must behold this unnatural contest with inexpressible anxiety. There never was a period in our history more critical than the present. It is high time some methods were adopted to conciliate these growing differences. The colonies are daily gaining incredible strength. They *know*, they *feel*, their importance; and *persuasion*, not *force*, must retain them in obedience.

A general nonimportation agreement will speedily take place, and I have reason to believe will be resolutely adhered to. It is therefore to be feared the manufacturers and artificers in Britain will be much distressed and probably driven to great extremities. For I need not observe to a man so conversant as you are with the commercial interests of the empire how severely the mother country must suffer by an interruption of her extensive trade with this continent. It is the universal doctrine *here* that it will plunge you into violent commotions and probably be attended with fatal consequences.*

A serious transaction took place, a few days since, in this city. The affair is partially represented in the *Maryland Gazette*. I attended the whole progress of the business, and was active in my exertions to prevent the extremities to which some frantic zealots proceeded.

On Saturday the fifteenth instant, the brig *Peggy Stewart* arrived from London with servants and an inconsiderable quantity of goods, among which were seventeen packages containing two thousand, three hundred, and twenty pounds of tea, consigned to Thomas Charles Williams and Company, merchants, in Annapolis. This intended importation was immediately discovered, and the citizens were summoned to a general meeting. On examination it appeared that Messrs. Williams had, on this occasion, imported a larger quantity of that detestable plant, as it is here termed, than by any former opportunity; and that Mr. Anthony Stewart, the proprietor of the vessel, had paid the duties thereon, though he was not in any shape concerned in the property. This was deemed a submission to the contested claim of the British parliament. Very severe censures were accordingly passed on

* The separation of America from Great Britain was contemplated, by persons of all descriptions, as pregnant with ruin to both countries. It must be granted that in consequence of this event very many deserving individuals have experienced a reverse of fortune which has subjected them to innumerable difficulties and distresses: but in a political point of view, this dreaded revolution has been attended with circumstances highly beneficial to the parent state. The superiority of the manufactures of Britain, and the established knowledge of her merchants in all the articles essential for the American market, have given them decided advantages over every rival nation. Similarity of language, customs, and opinions likewise powerfully operate in favor of the mother country; so that at this period, with every pleasing prospect of an uninterrupted continuation, Britain supports a more extensive and a more lucrative commerce with the United States than at any time during their immediate connection as a part of her empire.

the parties concerned, and a general spirit of resentment appeared to predominate. After various modes of proceeding had been proposed and discussed, it was determined to appoint a committee to attend the vessel and prevent the landing of the tea, until the sense of the county could be fully collected. The ensuing Wednesday was appointed for that purpose, and proper measures were pursued to give the necessary information.

Mr. Stewart, apprehensive of the consequences likely to ensue, with great propriety solicited a previous meeting of the citizens on the following Monday; trusting that, by a timely submission, measures might be taken to prevent the assembling of so numerous a body as were expected to come in from the country, from whom he had much to fear with respect to his person and his property.

At this meeting it was proposed by the moderate party that Messrs. Stewart and Williams, who were desirous to make atonement for the offense they had committed, might be permitted to land and burn the tea in any place that should be appointed for that purpose. This motion was, however, strongly opposed by others, who insisted on matters remaining as they were until the time appointed for the county meeting, in order that a more public acknowledgment and satisfaction might be made.

Mr. Stewart, with a view to moderate the resentment which his conduct had unhappily occasioned, distributed the following handbill and affidavit, which were also publicly read, but without any apparent effect in his favor.

To the Gentlemen of the Committee, the citizens of Annapolis, and the Inhabitants of Ann Arundel County.

Gentlemen,
I find by a handbill that you are requested to meet to take into consideration what is proper to be done with the tea, the property

of Thomas C. Williams and Co., now on board the brig *Peggy Stewart,* and finding my conduct censured for having paid the duty on that tea to the collector, I take the liberty to present a plain narrative of the part I have acted therein and the motives by which I was actuated. Deeply interested as I am in the peace and harmony of this country, no man would be farther than myself from taking any steps to disturb them. I am not in the least connected with anything that relates merely to the importation; indeed so cautious have I been of infringing in the least any of the resolutions of America that I did not order a single farthing's worth of goods by that vessel, though I could have done it on such easy terms as to freight and shipping charges; much less should I have thought of ordering any tea, after the disturbance which the importation of that article had occasioned on the continent. When the brig arrived, the captain informed me she was very leaky, and that the sooner she was unloaded the better. I told him to enter his vessel, but not the tea, which I found, on enquiry of the collector, could not be done. Under these circumstances, the brig leaky and fifty-three souls on board, where they had been near three months, I thought myself bound both in humanity and prudence to enter the vessel, and leave the destination of the tea to the committee. The impropriety of securing the duty did not then occur to me, neither did I know the tea would be suffered to be lodged as a security for the payment. I had nothing in view but to save the vessel from a seizure, and of having an opportunity of releasing the passengers from a long and disagreeable confinement. The duty on tea has been paid hitherto, both in Virginia and Maryland, by every importer of goods: in this case I am not the importer. If I have erred in my part of the transaction, I declare, upon my honor, it is without the least intention; I have infringed no rules prescribed by the general resolutions of this province. It happened unluckily that the tea was put on board of Captain Jackson's brig, in the manner as will be seen by the annexed affidavit; and it can be incontestably proved the captain refused taking tea on board:

Mr. Williams was in London when the tea was shipped and must have known that many merchants had refused to ship that article. I have only to add that I am sincerely sorry my conduct on this occasion has been the cause of so much uneasiness, and freely submit it to your candid consideration.

I am,
Gentlemen,

Annapolis,
October 17, 1774

Your most humble servant,
ANTHONY STEWART

AFFIDAVIT

Captain Richard Jackson, master of the brig *Peggy Stewart,* deposeth and saith, That immediately after the landing of his cargo in London he applied for and obtained a *general* permit from the custom house to receive *India and other goods* on board for exportation; and (as is always customary in such cases) gave security and took an oath not to reland the same in any part of Great Britain. But having great reason to believe any importation of tea would be unfavorably received in America, he was fully determined, and had resolved not to receive any on board; and publicly on the Change of London, in the month of July, refused to receive tea, which was offered to be shipped by Kelly, Lott, and Co. This deponent further saith, that by the method of shipping goods from London, *tea* may be put on board any ship, without the knowledge of the master. All goods are examined at the custom house, and sent by the shipper in lighters on board the ship, with only a common bill expressing the parcels and not the quantities contained or the qualities of them; these are received by the mate of the ship, who gives a receipt on the lighter bill, which is again returned to the shipper, and the master signs his bills of lading *at London,* by the lighter bill, specifying the parcels without knowing the contents, and clears out the ship at the custom house with merchandise without knowing or mentioning of what nature. The cockets containing the particulars of each parcel are sent by the officers of the customs at London to the custom house at Gravesend, and there lodged to be called for by the captain or master of the ship on his passage to sea. In this manner the goods shipped in the *Peggy Stewart* were received on board. And this deponent further saith that he saw

Thomas Charles Williams, to whom the tea is consigned, and Amos Hayton, who shipped the same, frequently in London, neither of whom ever mentioned to him their intention of shipping any; that he did not know of any tea being on board until after he had received his cockets at Gravesend, and that he would not have received the same had he known thereof.

RICH. JACKSON

Sworn before me, this } PHIL. THOS. LEE
October 17, 1774

On Wednesday the appearance, agreeable to expectation, was numerous; and the delegated committee were attended by Messrs. A. Stewart and Williams, who acknowledged the impropriety of their proceeding and signed the humiliating paper, of which the following is a copy.

We, James Williams, Joseph Williams, and Anthony Stewart, do severally acknowledge that we have committed a most daring insult and act of the most pernicious tendency to the liberties of America; we, the said Williams's, *in importing the tea,* and said Stewart, *in paying the duty thereon;* and thereby deservedly incurred the displeasure of the people now convened, and all others interested in the preservation of the constitutional rights and liberties of North America, do ask pardon for the same; and we solemnly declare for the future that we never will infringe any resolution formed by the people for the salvation of their rights; nor will we do any act that may be injurious to the liberties of the people; and to show our desire of living in amity with the friends of America, we request this meeting, or as many as may choose to attend, to be present at any place where the people shall appoint, and we will there commit to the flames, or otherwise destroy, as the people may choose, the detestable article which has been the cause of this our misconduct.

ANTHONY STEWART
JOSEPH WILLIAMS
JAMES WILLIAMS

Mr. Stewart, on account of what was deemed a cheerful and ready compliance with an unconstitutional act of the

British legislature, was particularly obnoxious: and though he publicly read his recantation, expressed in the most submissive and penitential terms, there were frantic zealots among the multitude who warmly proposed the American discipline of tarring and feathering. Others with a less vindictive spirit were clamorous for the destruction of the brig which had imported the hateful commodity; whilst many others, who indeed were the more numerous party, candidly declared "that the paper signed by the offenders, with their unextorted consent to burn the tea, was a sufficient punishment and satisfaction." But to determine this point with certainty, it was proposed and assented to that a division should take place on the following question: "Whether the vessel should or should not be destroyed?" When it was carried in the negative by a considerable majority, the citizens in general appearing averse to violent measures. But as the minority were chiefly persons who resided at a distance from Annapolis; as some of them had great influence in their neighborhood, and intimated a determined resolution to proceed to the utmost extremities, the instant they could collect sufficient numbers to support them Mr. Stewart was induced, from an anxious desire to preserve the public tranquility as well as to ensure his own personal safety, to propose setting fire himself to the vessel; which being immediately assented to, he instantly repaired on board, accompanied by several gentlemen who thought it necessary to attend him, and having directed her to be run on ground near the windmill point, he made a sacrifice of his valuable property to intemperate zeal and clamor; and in a few hours the brig, with her sails, cordage, and every appurtenance, was effectually burnt.[1]

By comparing the foregoing account with the circum-

[1] The burning of the *Peggy Stewart,* popular at the time, has since been commemorated annually as Peggy Stewart Day. Anthony Stewart named the brig after his young daughter, Peggy.

stances stated in the *Maryland Gazette,* a manifest difference appears. Every step that Messrs. Stewart and Williams took in this transaction to the prejudice of their property, seems, in that publication, to proceed from a voluntary election, unawed and unintimidated by the multitude; but I need not comment on the absurdity of such an opinion. The truth is they destroyed property of great value to prevent worse consequences.

Annapolis, November 2nd

The Congress have concluded their deliberations. I have seen their resolves, the association, the petition to his majesty, and the addresses to Great Britain, to Canada, and to the confederating American colonies.

The petition to the king is not to be published on this side the water until advice is received of its delivery at St. James. It was sent home from Philadelphia by a ship, which by this time, is probably far on its way. God knows what influence these papers may have in England. If they are supported by truth, may they produce effects to the mutual advantage of all parties! The petition is held to be a masterly performance, firm, explicit, and respectful; the address to Great Britain is thought to be pathetic and persuasive, that to Canada to be founded on sentiments of liberty and reason; and that to the uniting provinces to be instructive and moderating. I have perused them with impartial attention but am not competent to determine on their respective merits. It is evident the colonists are unanimous and will steadily support the proceedings of their delegates. Our printer is closely engaged at the press; the whole will make a tolerable pamphlet; and should the publication take place before this packet is dispatched, I shall forward it by the same conveyance.

I do not imagine the present situation of affairs will materially affect you, at least for some time; but I and mine are already too sensible of the evils attending the contest. My income is now considerably reduced; trade is already at a stand; and on the first of December, a general nonimportation takes place. Commodities of every kind are, at this early period, become scarce and dear. Neither money or bills can be found; and few people are sufficiently provided to answer the purposes of their necessary expenditure. Amidst every suffering, the reflection that thousands of industrious manufacturers at home must take their proportion of the impending calamity gives infinite disquietude to every honest and feeling mind.

The West Indies will likewise severely suffer, for without any share in political proceedings, they are doomed to a heavy punishment.

Annapolis, November 8th

The governor is returned to a land of trouble. He arrived about ten this morning in perfect health. He is now commenced an actor on a busy theater, his part a truly critical one. To stem the popular torrent and to conduct his measures with consistency will require the exertion of all his faculties. The present times demand superior talents; and his, I am persuaded, will be invariably directed to promote the general good. Hitherto his conduct has secured to him a well merited popularity; and his return to the province has been expected with an impatience which sufficiently evinces the sentiments of the public in his favor. May he be enabled to discharge his duties to the parent state and to the country over which he presides with unblemished credit and uninterrupted tranquility! Enclosed you have the proceedings of Congress, with an inflammatory pamphlet published at Boston. Whether the doctrine it contains corresponds with its title, *Common Sense,* I shall leave you to determine.[2]

[2] Eddis could not have referred to Paine's *Common Sense,* which was not issued until January 10, 1776, at Philadelphia. The likeliest explanation is that he wrote the last two sentences of this paragraph as they stand, except the words *Common Sense,* which he interpolated when he edited the letters for publication years later. By that time Paine's pamphlet had become famous and Eddis inserted the title feeling that the passage, otherwise rather cryptic, should be pointed up. His memory of the sequence of events played him false. Doubtless the pamphlet to which he referred, not by title in his original letter, was Charles Lee's *Strictures on a Pamphlet Entitled "Friendly Address to all Reasonable Americans, on the Subject of our Political Confusions"* which was published at Boston in 1775 and was widely reprinted in the colonies that year. Both the Proceedings of Continental Congress and "the latest political pamphlets" had been available at the bookstore of William Aikman at Annapolis since late May. *Maryland Gazette,* May 25, 1775.

LETTER XIX

There is but too much reason to apprehend that the hour is approaching when even the intercourse of letters will be greatly interrupted, if not totally prohibited.

From one extremity of this continent to the other every appearance indicates approaching hostilities. The busy voice of preparation echoes through every settlement; and those who are not zealously infected with the general frenzy are considered as enemies to the cause of liberty, and without regard to any peculiarity of situation are branded with opprobrious appellations and pointed out as victims to public resentment.

Very considerable subscriptions have been made in every quarter for the relief of the Bostonians: large sums have likewise been collected for the purchase of arms and ammunition, and persons of all denominations are required to associate under military regulations, on pain of the severest censure; every measure tending to the most fatal consequences is eagerly and wildly pursued.

Admitting the evils complained of to be founded on reality, the mode adopted to obtain redress cannot, in my opinion, be justified on principles of reason or sound policy. I have, therefore, refused to join in any of the proposed contributions, to appear in any of the associations, or to enroll in any military corps. I have even attempted to moderate the enthusiasm of intemperate zeal by the following appeal to common sense and common equity, which, through the medium of the *Maryland Gazette,* has been submitted to public inspection; and if favorable conclusions may be drawn from appearances, it has been received with considerable approbation, my letter having already been reprinted in almost every paper throughout this continent.

TO THE PRINTERS[1]

The present unhappy contention between the *mother country* and her *colonies* is a matter of the deepest concern to every honest, every feeling mind: it is, therefore, the indispensable duty of every friend to society to study and to pursue those methods which may lead to a perfect reconciliation and the establishment of a permanent union between *Great Britain* and *America.*

The principle of *parliamentary taxation* over this extensive part of the empire is generally denied by all ranks and denominations of men; the grand subject of controversy, therefore, that prevails at present, respects *the most eligible method to obtain redress.* On this point there appears a division of sentiment, which has given rise to *heart-burnings and discontent;* and in some degree struck at the root of that harmony which, at this important period, ought to *guide* and *influence* every action.

In opposition to measures dictated by *calmness* and *moderation* (a steady adherence to which, it was generally supposed, would be attended with the most happy effects), *a military appearance* is assumed — *subscriptions* are industriously making for the purchase of *arms, ammunition, etc.* and the *severest censure* is indiscriminately passed on those persons who happen to dissent from the popular opinion and prefer more conciliating methods of accommodation.

It is certain that there are many in *this* and other *provinces* who object to the spirit of violence, which seems at this time too predominant. Convinced of the propriety of their sentiments and the integrity of their hearts, they conceive the cause of America may be *totally injured* by a precipitate and unnecessary defiance of the power of Great Britain; they firmly believe that a respectful behavior to their *sovereign* and their *mother country* — a duti-

[1] The letter appeared in the issue dated February 16, 1775.

ful and constitutional application to the *throne* — and a firm perseverance in *virtuous* though *pacific principles* will, in the issue, be productive of the most felicitous consequences. Actuated by such considerations, they cannot be reconciled to those violent extremes which have been too rashly adopted by many, and which they are anxious to establish as the *only* feasible plan of terminating the present dissensions.

On deliberate reflection, it can hardly be imagined that the mother country has formed the least intention of reducing these provinces to a state of abject servility by the force of arms; the *natural connection* — the *close ties* — and *nice dependencies* which exist between the different parts of the empire forbid indulging any conclusions of so melancholy a nature. She will be more just — more tender to her offspring — the voice of reason will prevail — our grievances will be redressed — and she will be found, *to the end of time,* a kind — a fostering parent! But admitting that Great Britain were determined to enforce a submission to all her mandates; even in that case we have little cause to apprehend that she will *unsheath the sword* and establish her decrees in *the blood of thousands.* A more safe and certain method is obvious: a small proportion of *her naval power* would entirely shut up our harbors — suspend our trade — impoverish the inhabitants — promote intestine divisions — and involve us in all the horrors of anarchy and confusion. To avoid evils *even great as these,* we are not meanly to bend the neck and submit to every innovation. But when there is no prospect of such dreadful calamities, why are we to form ideas of *battles* and of *slaughter?* Why are our coasts to resound with *hostile preparations?* — the demon of *discord* to stalk at large — and *friends* and *kindred* forget the peaceful bonds of *amity* and *love?*

It has been objected by the advocates for moderation that the methods pursued to complete the subscription for arms, etc. has more the complexion of *an arbitrary tax* than *a voluntary contribution.* On the other hand, it has been asserted, that money raised in a manner where there is no obligation to pay but a sense of duty and no other mode to induce compliance but shame and infamy, cannot be deemed *a tax.* A sense of duty is, undoubtedly, the most noble incentive to *worthy actions;* but a false dread of *shame* and *infamy* has perverted many *an honest heart* and too frequently proved an irresistible temptation to *dishonorable practices*. Let us a moment reflect: Can there be an imposition more arbitrary and severe than a necessity of assenting to any particular measure, or forfeiting *that fair* — that *unsullied* — *reputation,* which alleviates the cares of life and smooths the inevitable rugged path to the dreary mansions of the grave!

    Good name in man and woman
Is the immediate jewel of their souls.
Who steals my purse, steals trash; 'tis something, nothing;
'Twas mine, 'tis his, and has been slave to thousands;
But he that filches from me my good name,
Robs me of that which not enriches him,
And makes me poor indeed.

If I differ in opinion from the multitude, must I therefore be deprived of my character and the confidence of my fellow citizens, when in every station of life I discharge my duty with fidelity and honor? DEATH, the certain tax on all the sons of men, were preferable to so abject a state. No — 'twere better to suffer all that "age, ache, penury, imprisonment, can lay on nature," than resign that glorious inheritance of a free subject — the liberty of *thinking, speaking,* and *acting,* agreeable to the dictates of conscience! I frankly acknowledge no man has a right to disturb the peace of the community by broaching tenets destructive to the *true interests* and *welfare* of his country; but at the same time, it cannot be justifiable to compel others to adopt *every system* which we esteem conducive to the public good. Let us therefore be unanimous in *virtue,* in *frugality,* and in *industry;* let us conduct ourselves on the Christian principle of "doing to others as we would have done to us"; let us not, in the frantic moments of intemperate zeal, mistake *libertinism* for *liberty,* and commit outrages which we shall recollect with *shame* and condemn with *heartfelt anxiety*. While we contend for the inestimable blessings of British subjects, let us not assume a *tyrannical authority* over each other. In a word, let *reason* and *moderation* hold the scale in every important determination — so shall every *real grievance* be effectually redressed — every man shall sing the song of gladness under his own *vine,* and we shall at once be free — be loyal — and be happy!

I am, Sir,

Most sincerely,

Annapolis,
February 14, 1775

A Friend to Amity

On perusing the above humble effort of my pen, it will readily occur to you that if I had, in the most distant manner, admitted the right of parliamentary taxation, my address, in times like these, could not possibly have been productive of any salutary consequences. The denial of that right being the prevailing creed of the colonies, I found myself necessitated to coincide with the popular opinion, that I might strike, with the greater efficacy, at that vindictive, arbitrary system, which under the fallacious pretense of supporting the interests of constitutional freedom, exerts a tyrannical authority in order to enforce hostile opposition in preference to moderate and respectful applications.

How far the legislative authority of Great Britain legally extends over the American provinces is beyond the extent of my limited abilities to determine. In the confidence of conversation, I daily hear various opinions, supported by strength of argument and accuracy of observation, and from what I have heard and am enabled to judge, I am clearly convinced that much more is apprehended than has any existence in reality. But in all countries there are busy, turbulent spirits who from motives of ambition, avarice, or discontent, "infect the general ear with horrid speech"; by eagerly pressing forwards, as champions in the public cause, they agitate the passions of the misguided multitude and imperceptibly lead them to the most dreadful extremities.

It is with pleasure I am able to assert that a greater degree of moderation appears to predominate in this province than in any other on the continent; and I am perfectly assured we are very materially indebted for this peculiar advantage to the collected and consistent conduct of our governor, whose views appear solely directed to advance the interests of the community and to preserve, by every possible method, the public tranquility. How long we may continue thus distinguished, time alone must determine. Should our demagogues obtain the ascendency after which they labor, we shall assuredly equal any of our neighbors in those violences of which we now only contemplate the commencement.

While the power of communicating my sentiments, *with safety,* is happily continued, I shall not fail to give you due information of every material circumstance.

LETTER XX

About noon this day arrived an express from Boston which brought an account, "that on the 19th instant a detachment of the king's troops, consisting of about a thousand men, being ordered on some secret duty at a place called Lexington, fell in with a company of provincials, whom they attacked without any provocation, killed six and wounded four; that on an alarm being given, the regulars were, in consequence, assaulted by a numerous body of the militia, who had surrounded them; and it was supposed the conflict would be desperate and bloody."

An additional paragraph says, "that General Gage[1] had sent a reinforcement, with some artillery, to sustain the troops; but that measures were taken to prevent their junction; that when the express was dispatched about one hundred and fifty soldiers were killed, and about fifty New Englandmen; and that the engagement continued with determined resolution."

With the most dreadful anxiety are we now waiting for further and more circumstantial intelligence.

The last advices from London intimate that both houses of parliament have addressed His Majesty, requesting him

[1] General Thomas Gage (1721-1787), governor of Massachusetts and commander-in-chief of British forces in the province, 1774-1775.

to enforce the acts; and that it has been determined, in consequence, to increase the army already in America.

I take it for granted this intelligence has brought on the commencement of hostilities, the violent party having conceived the practicability of reducing General Gage before he is rendered more formidable by the fresh supplies. Should the event be answerable to their expectation, the measure will be applauded by very many of the rash and inconsiderate. If they fail, the disappointment may probably give encouragement to the cool and moderate throughout the different provinces to exert their influence and their abilities in order to prevent the continent, in general, from participating in the miseries of war!

The provincial convention are now sitting in Annapolis, but strangers are not permitted to attend their debates. They have already dispatched an express to the southward in consequence of the information from Boston.

The plan proposed for a reconciliation, by Lord North, is generally approved by the moderate and dispassionate as the foundation of a permanent tranquility.* These men have ever been of opinion that the plantations ought to contribute more liberally than they at present do in return for

* On the motives and conduct of the American war there are various opinions, but only *one* exists with respect to the zeal evinced by the above nobleman in behalf of those who had freely sacrificed their all to their loyalty and to the British constitution.

The writer of these letters would be greatly wanting in gratitude were he not happy in this opportunity of acknowledging his particular obligations to the Earl of Guilford. At the time of his arrival in England, His Lordship was at the head of the Treasury, to whom he stated those circumstances which had compelled him to abandon his very eligible situations in the province of Maryland. The facts being properly authenticated, His Lordship was pleased, without the *most distant* interference of private interest and with a dispatch beyond the author's most sanguine expectations, to allot him a temporary provision, which enabled him to support with comfort that reverse of fortune which had rendered him dependent on the justice and humanity of his country.

the advantages of commerce and for the protection afforded by Great Britain. But how far His Lordship's conciliatory scheme may operate, now when actual hostilities are commenced, heaven alone can determine.

Thursday, April 27

Last night advice was received from Virginia that the powder and stores in the magazine at Williamsburg were taken from thence by some marines belonging to one of His Majesty's vessels on that station, by order of His Excellency Lord Dunmore.[2]

This intelligence has given an additional alarm to our patriotic party; and accordingly some gentlemen were deputed by the convention to wait on the governor, soliciting him to give directions that the arms, powder, and stores belonging to the province should be delivered into their possession, apprehensions being entertained "That some ship of war may arrive in the harbor of Annapolis whose commander might probably have instructions to seize the same."

The deputation was received with respect, and the governor promised to consult his council with all possible dispatch. This answer has given satisfaction for the present; and the militia, who were assembled to enforce submission, are departed quietly to their habitations.

April 28

To prevent riot and confusion, the governor and council have thought it advisable to comply with the requisition of the convention, on condition that the colonels of the militia in the respective counties under the ancient establishment solicit for the delivery of the arms, powder, and stores,

[2] John Murray, fourth Earl of Dunmore (1731-1809), governor of Virginia, 1772-1776.

pointing out the necessity of the measure. By this mode of proceeding the dignity of government is maintained and the public tranquility preserved. In these turbulent times something must be yielded to the clamor of an infatuated multitude.

The inhabitants of New York have hitherto discovered sentiments favorable to government; but if the sword is unsheathed, it is apprehended they will almost unanimously fall into the ranks of opposition. A report is circulated that fourteen regiments are ordered to that city, who are to prevent all communication between the southern and eastern provinces. In consequences of this rumor, their committee of observation have transmitted dispatches to Pennsylvania, Maryland, Virginia, and other places, desiring immediate assistance should such an event take place. How *our* patriots will act in this business I know not; for my part I suspect there are people who industriously circulate reports, and magnify the most trivial circumstances, with a view to inflame the minds of the multitude. Men of this complexion are best gratified when, by fomenting divisions and exciting apprehensions, they are enabled to take the lead in the subversion of all order, and by obtaining an iniquitous preeminence,

Ride in the tempest, and direct the storm.

Wednesday, May 3

We are incessantly alarmed with varied accounts from the northward full of inconsistency and contradiction; but upon the whole there is the greatest reason to conclude that the action between the regulars and provincials has not been attended with consequences so fatal as has been industriously represented. We are, however, still in the dark with respect to authentic particulars.

The governor last night received a circular letter from Lord Dartmouth,[3] with a resolution of the house of commons relative to a conciliatory plan. I pray God it may be attended with efficacy, though I fear the unhappy event at Lexington will retard the accomplishment of peace.

I am heartily disgusted with the times. The universal cry is *Liberty!* to support which, an infinite number of petty tyrannies are established, under the appellation of committees, in every one of which a few despots lord it over the calm and moderate, inflame the passions of the mob, and pronounce those to be enemies to the general good who may presume any way to dissent from the creed they have thought proper to impose.

Our provincial convention rose this day; and, considering the complexion of the times, their proceedings have been regular and moderate. The eleventh instant is to be observed as a fast throughout this province; the mustering is to be continued; and a sum is to be raised in each county for the support of the delegates in Philadelphia.

From the public prints it is difficult to form a clear idea of the prevailing opinion at home respecting the present unhappy and unnatural contention. If determined measures are pursued under officers of approved trust and ability, it can hardly be imagined that the colonies will be equal to a long and serious opposition; but whether a reduction of them by force would be attended with the desired consequences is a question that ought to be considered in preference to every other object. It will surely be advisable on the part of the British commanders to act only on defensive principles, until every lenient method has been adopted to restore harmony and mutual confidence on a constitutional foundation. It is evident there are too many individuals, in

[3] William Legge, second Earl of Dartmouth (1731-1801), from 1772 to 1775 secretary of state for colonies and president of the Board of Trade. Lord George Germain succeeded him in 1775.

every province, who from interested or ambitious motives embrace all opportunities to foment the seeds of division, by inflammatory addresses to the passions of the multitude, by repeated misrepresentations, and by artfully delineating the miseries of that arbitrary system which, they assert, will be the inevitable consequence of submission to ministerial mandates. Yet there are also, throughout this continent, many respectable characters whose real importance and established reputation give them such due weight and influence that I cannot but indulge the pleasing idea they will, by the steadiness and consistency of their conduct, be able to stem the torrent excited by factious artifices, and to forward measures that may be essential to the interests and happiness of the united British empire.

Supported by this hope, those who are sincerely attached to the prosperity and welfare of the general community direct their best attention to the parent state. Under the evils that now oppress them, they derive some consolation from a firm persuasion that the olive branch will speedily be extended, and that such wise and judicious dispositions will be made for future legislation in the colonies that many inestimable advantages will arise from past and present calamities.

May 13

At length we have received General Gage's account of the late action, which is materially different from those transmitted by the respective committees, and, I think, may be more certainly relied on, being written ten days after the engagement, when the particulars relative to the whole transaction were properly and minutely collected. The charge of cruelty and precipitation is now retorted on the provincials. But the patriots yield no credit to this relation, though they affect to believe implicitly every report propagated to the disadvantage of the British forces.

The members of the Congress are now assembled in Philadelphia.[4] I need not say with what anxiety we attend the event of their deliberations. The governor continues to stand fair with the people of this province; our public prints declare him to be the only person in his station who in these tumultuous times has given administration a fair and impartial representation of important occurrences; and I can assert with the strictest regard to truth that he conducts himself in his arduous department with an invariable attention to the interests of his royal master and the essential welfare of the province over which he has the honor to preside.

[4] Eddis refers here to the second Continental Congress.

LETTER XXI

Annapolis, July 25, 1775

Mr. D—— will do me the favor to deliver this letter. He is going to pass some time on the continent of Europe, where he hopes to find that tranquility which is not at present to be obtained in this unhappy country. I shall leave him to represent minutely the calamitous situation of the colonies. Government is now almost totally annihilated, and power transferred to the multitude. Speech is become dangerous; letters are intercepted; confidence betrayed; and every measure evidently tends to the most fatal extremities; the sword is drawn, and without some providential change of measures the blood of thousands will be shed in this unnatural contest.

Before this letter is received, you will have heard of the action at *Bunker's Hill*. The provincials were forced from their entrenchments; but it is said the regulars suffered so severely that they cannot afford to obtain future advantages at so dear a price.

The inhabitants of this province are incorporated under military regulations, and apply the greater part of their time to the different branches of discipline. In Annapolis there are two complete companies; in Baltimore seven; and in every district of this province the majority of the people are actually under arms; almost every hat is decorated with a cockade; and the churlish drum and fife are the only music of the times.

I have not yet, in positive terms, been required to muster; and I trust my peculiar circumstances will be considered as

113

a reasonable plea of exemption. I wish well to America. It is my duty — my inclination so to do — but I cannot — I will not — consent to act in direct opposition to my oath of allegiance and my deliberate opinion. Rather than submit to a conduct so base, so inconsistent with my principles, I will give up all — embrace ruin! — and trust to the protecting care of Providence for the future disposition of me and mine.

On Tuesday the 18th instant, a number of armed persons set fire to a ship which had accidentally run on ground a few miles below this city. She was the property of Mr. Gildart of Liverpool, and had brought in some goods contrary to the association. This is the second burnt offering to liberty within this province; at the same time, it is but justice to confess that these instances of popular fury are heartily condemned by very many, even of the patriotic party.

Mr. James C[hristie],[1] a respectable merchant of Baltimore, lately addressed a letter to a near relation, Lieutenant Colonel C[hristie] of the 60th regiment, stationed in the island of Antigua, in which he strongly expressed his disapprobation of the prevailing system. This letter has been intercepted and laid before the committee of Baltimore county; and on its being made public, his house was surrounded by a disorderly rabble, and had not a detachment of the militia interfered, Mr. Christie would probably have fallen a sacrifice. This gentleman is now a close prisoner, under the custody of a guard, and his case is to be laid before the provincial convention, who meet tomorrow in this city for the purpose of establishing new regulations.

The proclamation issued by General Gage is very little regarded. Hancock and Adams are therein excepted from mercy! The Congress have adjourned until September.

My friend M—— arrived on the 18th and delivered your

[1] James Christie, later a Loyalist, wrote Lieutenant Colonel Gabriel Christie the letter referred to here. Parts of the letter are printed in *Archives of Maryland*, II (*Proceedings of the Convention*), 44-45.

circumstantial epistle. How we are to correspond hereafter I know not. On the tenth of September next the nonexportation association takes place, and all commercial intercourse will consequently cease until these unhappy differences are by some means decided. It seems but yesterday that I considered my situation as permanent. Every flattering prospect appeared before me. Happy in my family, in my connections, in my circumstances, cherished and supported by a patron able and anxious to promote my interest. Alas! my brother, how cruelly is the scene reversed! I am suddenly involved in a train of difficulties and dangers against which no human prudence or foresight could possibly guard. How strangely complicated have been the events of my life, on which, apparently, my own conduct has had so little influence. Under all circumstances believe me ever yours.

LETTER XXII

Annapolis, August 24, 1775

On the fourteenth instant, the convention concluded their deliberations. If their proceedings are published before I have an opportunity to transmit this, I will enclose them for your information. You will then be enabled to form an opinion of the disposition of this province.

When you have perused the association of the freemen of Maryland you will, I presume, acknowledge the propriety of my objecting to subscribe to it, and acknowledge that such conduct would be inconsistent with my principles and the station under government in which I am situated. I verily believed some regard would have been paid to the particular circumstances of revenue officers, but our present rulers entertain different sentiments, and all persons, without exception, must associate and enroll, the governor and his household *only* excepted.

His Excellency, ever attentive to my interest, has generously made me an offer to become one of his family, immediately after the embarkation of Mrs. Eddis, who is now anxiously preparing for her approaching voyage. We had firmly determined that no circumstances, however adverse to our hopes, should induce us again to consent even to a temporary separation; but the cruel necessity of our once more submitting to it has of late appeared too evident. She is perfectly convinced that I must speedily avow my political

sentiments in the most explicit manner, and that my refusal
to join in the popular measures will subject me to inconveniences which may better be supported when my family is
removed to some secure asylum. Influenced by such forcible
considerations, she has acknowledged the expediency of
what is so distressing to our domestic happiness! and early
in the ensuing month we must bid farewell! — a painful farewell to each other!

The governor's humane and generous offer impresses my
mind with the most lively gratitude; yet am I greatly embarrassed how to conduct myself on the occasion. Considering the wild, unsettled times, he is uncommonly popular;
but how long he may continue so is a matter of great uncertainty. It is highly probable he may speedily think it necessary to express his decided disapprobation of the present proceedings, which step, I am fearful, would effectually cancel
his past merits, subject him to calumny and censure, and
render his longer continuance in Maryland impossible.
Should the event prove these conjectures to be well
founded, I cannot possibly expect protection from the
friendly attention of my worthy patron; on the contrary, I
must either bid adieu to America, and every pleasing prospect, or meanly comply with the requisitions of the convention, in direct opposition to the sentiments of my heart. Let
me weigh both evils, with a settled determination to make
that election which will hereafter be attended with the
most salutary effects and the most pleasing reflections.

If I abandon this country in consequence of a steady adherence to my principles and my duty, I must unavoidably be
subjected to a precarious life of uncertainty and dependence;
and instead of enjoying a comfortable asylum in my native
land, I may only experience a variety of misfortunes and disappointments, and drink yet deeper draughts of the cup of
affliction. I am, however, perfectly assured, if I preserve my

integrity unblemished, though I should thereby be subjected to

— the spurns
That patient merit of the unworthy takes,

yet, hereafter, I shall receive an adequate reward.

On the other hand, should I act in opposition to the dictates of my mind, by subscribing to the association and taking arms, I shall not only be subject to those painful feelings which accompany a consciousness of doing wrong, but be justly despised by every brave and honest man; detested and avoided by every respectable society, and when tranquility is happily restored, deservedly cast out, to encounter a complication of miseries without one cheering thought to support such a reverse of fortune.

I have now fairly stated my situation; and believe from your knowledge of my principles you will readily determine how I shall regulate my conduct; and whenever I am unhappily necessitated to quit this country, where I have experienced great blessings, this pleasing reflection will accompany me, that I have left behind me a fair and unblemished reputation.

A new emission of paper currency, to the amount of sixty thousand pounds sterling, is now preparing under the inspection of gentlemen appointed by authority of the convention, which is hereafter to be sunk by a tax on the inhabitants of this province; besides which, they are to be assessed their proportion to sink the Congress money, amounting to six-hundred-and-seventy-five-thousand pounds, lately emitted at Philadelphia, for the payment of the provincial army. How these enormous expenses are to be supported, and how the people are to be maintained, after a total stagnation of commerce, is not easy to conceive. If ways and means are not speedily devised to feed the hungry and clothe

the naked, we must assuredly experience all the horrors of the most extreme indigence.

Numbers of my valued friends are now preparing to bid farewell to a country, where they cannot possibly remain with any degree of safety unless they take an active part in opposition to the measures of government: to be neuter is to be adverse. What a variety of circumstances combine to make me wretched! It is but too probable that *I* also shall soon abandon this continent, either by sentence of banishment or by voluntary retreat. I cannot be excelled by any in good wishes to America, and I heartily pray that every real evil under which she labors may be speedily and effectually redressed; but the present measures will never meet my concurrence; I cannot subscribe to a compact which I believe to be incompatible with my oath of allegiance; nor can I think it consistent with that liberty which is the universal cry to compel any man to act in direct opposition to his well grounded principles.

I have written you a gloomy letter, which a word or two more shall conclude. In a former epistle, I mentioned Mr. James Christie, and the danger to which he was subjected in consequence of having imparted his opinions too explicitly in confidential correspondence. That gentleman has been examined by the convention, and there are vindictive spirits who think the sentence he has received by no means adequate to the *supposed* enormity of his offense. He has been pronounced

an enemy to America; condemned to perpetual banishment; and obliged to deposit the sum of five hundred pounds sterling, in the hands of persons appointed by the convention, to be expended occasionally towards his proportion of all charges incurred, or to be incurred, for the defense of America during the present contest with Great Britain; the overplus, if any, after a reconciliation shall happily be effected, to be restored to the said James Christie.

From this you will learn how hazardous it is become to support a free intercourse. The convention have thus assumed the powers of all the different branches of government; but with what propriety, it becomes not me to determine. That the blessings of peace may speedily be restored, is the fervent prayer of your faithful, etc.

LETTER XXIII

Annapolis, September 26, 1775

I am seated, my dearest wife, to transmit a detail of material occurrences since our unhappy separation on the sixteenth instant.

It is impossible to delineate the anguish I experienced when I quitted the vessel which was to convey you and our darling boy to a land of safety. Anxious to retain you as long as possible in my possession, I had proceeded with you further down the Bay than prudence warranted, and the night was far advanced before I regained the mansion of the hospitable colonel. I then retired to the apartment you had so recently quitted and gave a loose to all the complicated emotions which "harrowed up my soul."

On the nineteenth, the wind being favorable, I took leave of the worthy family at Rousby Hall and embarked for Annapolis. In my way down the river I visited a vessel which had anchored near the mouth on the preceding evening, and found on board several of our valued acquaintance, who had abandoned their dearest connections rather than assent to measures they could not conscientiously support.

Immediately on landing, I repaired to my new abode at the governor's, who received me with that friendly attention which so remarkably distinguishes his conduct on every occasion. I found him in company with a few select loyal friends; political occurrences engrossed our conversation, in which hope appeared to operate but weakly with respect to the eventful transactions of the times. At an early hour we separated; my apartment was ready for my reception; and after invoking Heaven on behalf of my wife and son, I rested with tolerable composure.

Mr. L——, who had actually embarked for England with full permission from the ruling powers, has been obliged to relinquish his intention and return on shore, some clamors have been excited by the populace to his prejudice, and it being thought necessary he should remain to vindicate his conduct. Many of our friends have found it expedient to take a French leave. I trust you will speedily meet them in perfect safety.

On the twentieth, I visited our once happy mansion. This was an additional trial of resignation and fortitude, every surrounding object too forcibly reminding me of past felicity. Your servants showed the strongest sensibility; and their earnest and pathetic inquiries relative to their dear mistress and our beloved boy proved the fervency and sincerity of their attachment. In a few days they remove to their respective situations. What a dreadful reverse have I already experienced!

September 26, P.M.

About an hour since, the governor was exceedingly surprised by the receipt of a letter from Mr. L[loyd] D[ulany][1] dated from Philadelphia. The contents intimate that on the tenth and eleventh instant they encountered a most violent storm about sixty leagues to the eastward of Virginia, during which the *Annapolis* lost all her masts; and that they continued three days in that dangerous situation before they were able to fix jury masts, under which they made sail for

---

[1] Lloyd Dulany (1742-1782), son of Daniel Dulany the elder by his third wife Henrietta Maria. Eden and his associates had particular concern for Lloyd's well-being because he carried a portfolio of confidential reports from Eden to Dartmouth.

the coast of America. On Tuesday, the nineteenth, they had the good fortune to fall in with a vessel bound to Philadelphia, which received the passengers and conveyed them to that city. Captain H[anrick] intends to go into the first port he can make in order to repair his damages, which are considerable. I need not observe that we wait for intelligence of his arrival with great anxiety.

We once considered the circumstances which prevented your sailing in that ship as a very severe disappointment; but in consequence of that seeming evil, what inconveniences, what terrors, have you not happily avoided! what increased expense! which in our present situation we are little able to support.

Wednesday evening, September 27

This morning early we were alarmed by the beating of drums and a proclamation for the inhabitants to assemble at the Liberty Tree. The purport of this meeting was to obtain a resolve, "That all persons who had refused to sign the association, and comply with the other requisitions, should be obliged to quit the city, as enemies to the essential interests of America." I have, however, the pleasure to inform you that this violent project was defeated with little difficulty; every judicious and reasonable person seeing through the pernicious tendency of such a design, and the promoters, who were amongst the lowest of the people, not being supported or encouraged. It is needless to mention that this proceeding was directly opposite to the resolves of the convention, it having been determined by that body that *they only* were competent to take cognizance of offenses and to ascertain the punishment.

I am, however, clearly of opinion that all power will quickly be transferred into the hands of the multitude, who once taking the lead will not easily be reduced again to proper submission. In some counties they have had warm contests in electing their delegates for the ensuing convention and in appointing members of the respective committees. In Talbot, the poll lasted several days; party prejudices were highly predominant, and much ill blood produced.

Mr. R[andolph],[2] the attorney general of Virginia, with his lady and daughters, are on their passage to England. His son is of the adverse party, and is appointed an aide-de-camp to General Washington, with whom, beneath the hospitable roof of our worthy governor, I have so frequently shared the hour of social and sentimental discourse. Little did I then conceive that he was destined to be called forth, by the united voice of America, from the private occupations of domestic tranquility to direct hostile operations against the measures of the British government. Reserved in conversation but liberal in opinion, his actions have hitherto been directed by calmness and moderation, a perseverance in which conduct may restrain misguided ardor and direct every movement to that grand point, a permanent and constitutional reconciliation.

The exaltation of this gentleman to the supreme command is considered as a severe stroke to the ambition of General Lee,[3] who, relying on a supposed opinion of his superior abilities and experience, expected to have been unanimously chosen to this elevated station. I am persuaded that General Washington would rejoice in an opportunity of returning into the private walks of life; but it is too evident that General Lee is governed by a vindictive spirit, the

[2] John Randolph (c. 1727/28-1784) succeeded his brother Peyton as attorney general in 1766. He was burgess from the College of William and Mary after 1774. In 1775 Randolph sided with Dunmore and left Virginia in the late summer for England where he spent the remainder of his life in exile.

[3] Major General Charles Lee (1731-1782), ex-officer of the British army who settled in Virginia and espoused the patriot cause. The Continental Congress appointed him major general on June 17, 1775.

result of disappointment in military advancement while in the service of Great Britain. Perhaps this additional mortification may moderate his zeal in the cause he had recently espoused.

The council of safety have given directions to several gentlemen in public departments to hold themselves in readiness to remove their books and papers. Intimations of this nature have not yet extended to myself or colleague, but when the convention meet it is expected we shall be included in whatever regulations they may think necessary to establish.

The report of a ship of war being ordered to this port has occasioned many families to quit Annapolis; and others talk of removing speedily. I have, however, the pleasure of informing you that the generality of the inhabitants seem perfectly disposed to conduct themselves with moderation, should such ship arrive; for at a respectable meeting of the citizens, on Monday last, it was unanimously agreed, "If a vessel belonging to His Majesty should be stationed in our harbor, to supply the same with every necessary at a reasonable price, and cautiously to avoid any cause of contention with the officers or the crew." An address is also prepared to be delivered to the governor expressive of these laudable sentiments, and entreating that he will intimate the same to the commander of any ship that may be ordered on this duty.

I shall be truly impatient till I learn that you are safely arrived. May the wished-for intelligence be soon conveyed to your ever faithful, etc

LETTER XXIV

Annapolis, November 16, 1775

When we parted, I intimated an intention of making an excursion to the northward, but on reflection think it prudent, during these discordant times, to relinquish the design. The city of New York is deserted by almost every respectable family, and Philadelphia only presents a view of military arrangements and general confusion. While the country is in such commotion, commerce and agriculture at a stand, and marks of distress, real or imaginary, imprinted on every countenance, it is absolutely impossible to receive any satisfaction from change of situation.

The King's proclamation and the Manchester address have appeared in the continental papers; but as I carefully avoid "the busy haunts of men," I am not sufficiently informed to determine on their general reception. From what I casually learn they do not tend to conciliate.

Friday, November 17

I have just received intelligence which gives me great disquietude. The September packet is arrived from England, but the letters are detained for inspection. The governor is much chagrined on the occasion.

Mrs. Washington, accompanied by her son, Mr. Custis,[1] and his lady, passed through Baltimore this day on their

---

[1] John Parke (Jackie) Custis (c. 1753-1781), son of Martha Washington by her first husband.

way to the camp at Cambridge, escorted by a detachment of horse that made a very military appearance.

Tuesday, November 21

The governor this morning received his letters, but they have passed the ordeal of examination. Those you may write to me will assuredly share the same fate. It is a painful reflection that private correspondence cannot escape being subjected to public investigation; but we must yield with resignation to the complexion of the times.

Annapolis is daily more and more deserted; some families have quitted us from apprehensions of a bombardment; others on account of the distressed times, bad markets, and a general scarcity of money; even tradesmen and mechanics have quitted their habitations, and are retired from the vicinity of navigable waters. Agriculture is neglected; the voice of peaceful industry is heard no more; and the military science is the universal study, so that I have, every hour, additional reason to felicitate myself on your absence from this wretched country.

Monday, November 27

A handbill is just arrived from the northward which conveys information that the metropolis of Canada has surrendered to Colonel Arnold,[2] by the reduction of which an immense quantity of military stores has fallen into the possession of the captors. The account says fifteen thousand stand of arms and two thousand five hundred barrels of gunpowder, with cannon, mortars, etc. Fifteen thousand suits of

---

[2] Benedict Arnold (1741-1801), hero of Ticonderoga, led American forces across the Maine wilderness to assault Quebec. The report that Quebec had surrendered proved false, as Eddis acknowledges later.

soldiers' clothing are also said to be included in this valuable capture. General Carleton[3] is at Montreal, but with what force is not ascertained; it is however imagined that place must inevitably fall, and the gallant commander submit to the provincial armament. War between different nations is an evil of great magnitude; but between people who acknowledge the same sovereign, who speak the same language, profess the same religion, and who are connected with each other by all the affecting ties of nature and of interest, it is indeed too horrible for imagination to conceive.

In consequence of the late success, our patriots talk in a strain of high exultation, and prognosticate events fatal to the political and commercial interests of the parent state.

As it is impossible during these unsettled times to conjecture what fortune may befall me, I would have you be constantly prepared for my arrival in London, as it may not be in my power to transmit you any information previous to my leaving this country. For if peace is not reestablished during the course of the present winter, I can neither enjoy happiness nor derive any advantage by remaining in America.

These wretched times indeed strike at the root of every home-felt enjoyment; every countenance is darkened with anxiety and suspicion; mutual confidence is annihilated; political prejudices erase the remembrance of former attachments, and friends and kindred forget the endearing bonds of amity and love.

December 3

The account of Quebec being taken appears to be premature, but sanguine expectations are entertained that it must speedily submit. Montreal has surrendered to General Mont-

[3] General Guy Carleton, first Lord Dorchester (1724-1808), governor of Canada and after 1782 commander-in-chief in America.

gomery.[4] The terms of capitulation will probably reach England long before this letter. These successes induce some people to look further than the original plan of opposition.

I charge you let not any solicitude on my account agitate your mind — let us not "shape the fashion of uncertain evils" — but reflecting on the *past* look forward confidently to the *future*.

[4] General Richard Montgomery (1738-1775) led American forces up the lake and river line to Canada and did take Montreal on November 13, 1775. He died at the battle of Quebec, December 31, 1775.

LETTER XXV

Annapolis, January 1, 1776

Were I to yield to those corroding reflections that naturally and irresistibly impress the mind under the peculiarly distressing circumstances of this distracted empire, I should assuredly form the most calamitous ideas respecting the events which may, too probably, take place before the commencement of a future year. Numbers of those with whom I have been connected on terms of amity and friendship are now the avowed and determined enemies of my much loved native country! — the reflection that they derived their being from the same original source appears almost entirely obliterated, and they are rushing impetuously forward into all the complicated dangers and miseries of hostile opposition. Multitudes who at this moment are distinguished by the endearing appellations of husbands! fathers! sons! and brethren! will assuredly, before the return of this day, exist only in the memory of those to whom they are now united by all the tender bonds of nature and attachment. From contemplating the general wreck, the mind irresistibly adverts to private sufferings.

> How richly were our noontide traces hung
> With gorgeous tapestries of pictur'd joys;
> Joy behind joy, in endless perspective.

What an unexpected, unavoidable reverse have we experienced! Our domestic felicity is sacrificed; our reasonable and well founded hopes of uninterrupted prosperity are cruelly frustrated, and every future view is dreary and calamitous. But it is possible all may yet be well. Tranquility may be effectually restored; we may be happily reunited and enabled to enjoy the residue of our days under a constant sense of that gracious providence which, through paths of danger, conducts to peace and safety and erects permanent happiness on the foundation of sorrow and disappointment.

For some time I have indulged the idea that the November packet would convey the pleasing intelligence of your safe arrival in London, and that you were enjoying as much satisfaction as the restoration of health and the attention of kind friends could possibly afford. But, alas! I am miserably disappointed by the painful information that from October last no more packets were to be dispatched regularly from England. It is, therefore, now become a doubt whether I shall obtain information of your welfare until it pleases heaven to restore you and our dearest child to my impatient arms.

Since your departure what a strange alteration has taken place. Our harbors — our rivers are deserted. The cheerful sound of industry is heard on more; activity is only exerted in warlike preparations; every visage is clouded with apprehension; and a continued succession of aggravated reports agitate the mind and foment the general discontent. Were my duty and my inclination reconcilable with each other, you would speedily behold me in England; but every motive of principle and affection equally operates to deny the gratification of my fondest wishes. For while a possibility remains that a reconciliation may be constitutionally effected between Great Britain and her colonies, it is undoubtedly incumbent on the servants of government not to relinquish their respective situations. Such conduct would be justly reprehensible, as it might occasion infinite irregularity and confusion, which by a decent and steady perseverance

may be avoided. I am persuaded these reasons will have
their due influence on your mind, and in a great degree prepare you to encounter those evils which I would even yet
hope are but temporary.

My dearest — my best — friend, farewell! Remember we
must endure to conquer

LETTER XXVI

Affairs in Virginia have borne for some time a very serious aspect. On the 25th of October last, Lord Dunmore cannonaded Hampton, a commercial town on the banks of the Chesapeake, but was repulsed with the loss of some men and a tender, which was taken by the militia. In consequence of this transaction, on the 7th of November a proclamation was issued by His Lordship, dated on board the ship *William* lying off Norfolk, declaring,

that as the civil law was insufficient at that period to prevent and punish treason, martial law should take place, and be executed throughout the colony, therefore requiring all persons capable of bearing arms to repair to his majesty's standard or to be considered as traitors. He also declared all indented servants, negroes, or others appertaining to persons in opposition to government, who were able and willing to bear arms, and who joined his majesty's forces, to be free.

This measure of emancipating the negroes has excited an universal ferment, and will, I apprehend, greatly strengthen the general confederacy.

The proclamation, however, had some immediate effect in the opulent town of Norfolk, where many of the inhabitants were well affected to government. The governor was speedily joined by some hundreds of all complexions, and he doubtless formed an idea that the disposition to loyalty which he discovered in that neighborhood would have been sufficiently general for enabling him to raise a force competent to reestablish what he deemed a proper degree of subordination.

This delusive expectation was interrupted by information that a party of provincials, under the command of Colonel Woodford,[1] were on their march to oppose his measures. To obstruct their progress and to support those who were well affected, Lord Dunmore immediately took possession of a post called the Great Bridge, some miles distant from Norfolk, which is a pass of great consequence and the only practicable way of approaching that town. Both parties fortified themselves within cannon shot of each other; and as a narrow causeway lay between them, which must necessarily be passed previous to an attack, they appeared to be mutually secured from any danger of surprise.

Thus circumstanced, they continued inactive several days, till at length a design was formed of surprising the American troops in their entrenchments. Captain Fordyce,[2] a very gallant officer at the head of about sixty grenadiers, led the attack; they passed the causeway with the utmost intrepidity, and with fixed bayonets rushed on an enemy who were properly prepared for their reception; for Captain Fordyce's party were not only exposed, naked, to a heavy fire in front, but were enfiladed from another part of the works. The brave leader, with several of his men, fell; the lieutenant, with the residue, all of whom were severely wounded, were taken prisoners.

The fire of the artillery from the British fort enabled the forces under the command of the governor to retreat from the post which they had occupied and which was now no

[1] Colonel William Woodford, later a general in the War for Independence, led the patriot sortie to oust Dunmore from Norfolk.

[2] Captain Charles Fordyce led this suicidal charge across a bridge (Great Bridge) spanning a marsh into which South Branch of the Elizabeth River flows. He lost about one hundred of his one hundred and twenty regulars as well as his own life.

longer tenable, without pursuit; and as all hopes in this quarter were terminated by the defeat, Lord Dunmore thought it expedient to abandon the town and neighborhood of Norfolk and retire on board the shipping, with numbers of persons who have been active in supporting his measures found it necessary to seek the same asylum. A considerable number of vessels was, by this means, collected, crowded with people and effects, but possessing little force and in great want of able mariners. The provincials immediately took possession of Norfolk, and the governor, with his adherents, removed to a greater distance.

The loyalists who had taken refuge in the fleet, together with the seamen and military, quickly became sensible of many difficulties and hardships, provisions, necessaries, and every kind of succor being absolutely denied from the adjacent shore. The ships likewise being constantly annoyed by the fire of the Americans from that part of the town which lay nearest the water, it was determined to dislodge them by destroying it. A flag, however, was first sent on shore to learn "whether the provincials would regularly supply His Majesty's ships with water and provisions," which requisition being answered in the negative, extremities were resolved on. Previous notice being acccordingly given that the inhabitants might remove to situations of security, the first day of the present year was signalized by the attack, when a violent cannonading commenced from the *Liverpool* frigate, two sloops of war, and the governor's armed ship, the *Dunmore,* supported by parties of the sailors and marines who landed and set fire to the nearest houses. These measures soon produced the intended effect, but not without the destruction of the whole town, which by the rapid progress of the flames was quickly reduced to ashes.

I have seen the copy of a gazette which was printed on board the governor's ship, he having removed the press and materials thither from Norfolk, in which it is confidently, and with great probability asserted, "that it was only intended to destroy that part of the town which adjoined the river, but that the provincials completed the devastation by setting fire to the remote streets, which, as the wind then stood, would otherwise have been secure from danger."

Such has been the fate of the most considerable commercial town in the colony of Virginia; and the whole loss upon the occasion is estimated at above three hundred thousand pounds. This unhappy event has given a fresh alarm to our citizens, many of whom are preparing to quit Annapolis.

The provincial assembly have been sitting here ever since the fourth of December. It is expected they will speedily adjourn.

Our governor is in perfect health. He still continues to receive every external mark of attention and respect; while the steady propriety of his conduct, in many trying exigencies, reflects the utmost credit on his moderation and understanding.

My ignorance of your situation is a very considerable addition to the disquietude I experience on account of public calamities. May my next acknowledge the receipt of an epistle from her who occupies every thought and whose happiness is the primary object I have in view! Under all the dispensations of Providence I shall remain unalterably yours

LETTER XXVII

The inhabitants of this city have been exceedingly alarmed. On the fifth instant, about eight in the evening, intelligence was received that a ship of war was on her passage up the bay, and at no great distance from Annapolis. The consternation occasioned by this information exceeds description. The night was tempestuous, extremely dark, and the rain descended in torrents, notwithstanding which many persons began to remove their effects; and the streets were quickly crowded with carriages laden with furniture and property of various kinds. A little reflection must have made it evident that without violent provocation, hostilities would not have commenced; and at all events, that timely notice would have been given previous to any bombardment. It ought to have been considered that a governor, acting under the authority of Great Britain, was resident in the town and apparently exercising the powers with which he was invested. No complaint had been transmitted on his part relative to the treatment experienced by him and the adherents of administration. His prudent and consistent conduct had greatly tended to prevent personal outrages; and under such circumstances it was manifest that no commander in His Majesty's service could have formed the most distant idea of proceeding to extremities without communicating his intentions to the supreme magistrate, who was undoubtedly a valuable pledge in the hands of the people, to secure themselves and property from immediate violence

But as reason seldom operates under instantaneous impressions, the governor resolved to pursue every eligible method that might effectually remove the apprehensions so universally entertained. Actuated by such motives, he made immediate application to the council of safety, and in order to dissipate the general anxiety proposed sending a flag of truce on board His Majesty's ship the instant she made her appearance or came to an anchor off the harbor. An offer so evidently tending to preserve the public tranquility was accepted with every suitable acknowledgment; and on the seventh instant, a ship of war accompanied by a tender passing by Annapolis, I had the honor to be deputed to perform this service; on which occasion I thought it necessary, in order to obviate any misrepresentation, to transcribe as follows the substance of my negotiation for the inspection of the governor, the council of safety, and the committee of observation.

Friday, March 8

By order of His Excellency the governor and with the approbation of the president of the council of safety, I repaired yesterday on board His Majesty's sloop, the *Otter,* commanded by Captain Squire, then lying at an anchor in Chesapeake Bay between Magotty River[1] and the Bodkin; and delivered to him a letter from the governor, to which a satisfactory answer was returned and immediately made known for the general information of the citizens of Annapolis.

In conversation with Captain Squire, I took occasion to expatiate on the temper and moderation of the people of Maryland;

---

[1] In the eighteenth century the Magothy River almost always went by the unlovely name Magotty. The Bodkin (now Bodkin's Point) is the needle-like projection at the south side of the entrance to the Patapsco River. In other words, the *Otter* anchored about half way between Annapolis and Baltimore where the captain could watch movement of ships at both.

their attachment to the British constitution; and their settled aversion to any design of establishing an independency: for an assurance of which I referred him to the instructions given to their delegates in Congress and to the proceedings of the late convention.

I informed Captain Squire that from the commencement of these unhappy dissentions, the governor and his friends had been treated with respect and attention; I recommended the utmost moderation in the execution of his orders; and assured him that in so doing the esteem of the people would be so far conciliated as to render the Maryland station as convenient and agreeable as the nature of the times would admit.

Captain Squire on his part explicitly acquainted me that it was the furthest from his intentions to proceed to any extremities; that he was instructed to demand a privateer, avowedly fitted out at Baltimore for hostile purposes; as also some vessels laden with flour, of which the navy were in the greatest want; that he was ready to pay the market price for any provisions that the inhabitants would supply him with, but otherwise he was under an absolute necessity to seize whatever might come within his power. Captain Squire promised that, if his requisitions were complied with, not the least damage should ensue to any individual or to the town of Baltimore.

Captain Squire mentioned that he had given particular directions to the gentlemen under his command not to fire under any pretext upon such persons as might assemble on the adjacent shores, or permit any depredations, but to perform such duty only as was absolutely essential to His Majesty's service.

Captain Squire from the whole of his behavior discovered the utmost concern for the unhappy breach which had taken place between the mother country and her colonies; and obliged as he was to act in the line of his duty, it appeared his most earnest wish to avoid any measures which might only tend to widen the calamitous dissention.

To the above I have only to add that my business on board was to recommend temperate proceedings, and to obtain such intelligence as might conduce to remove the apprehensions of the much alarmed citizens of Annapolis, in which service I have the satisfaction to believe I have not been altogether unsuccessful.

W. E.

Early in the afternoon the armed vessel of which they were in quest appeared in sight. The tender belonging to the sloop of war had proceeded further up the bay and had taken possession of a ship with a valuable cargo then lying at an anchor and ready for sea: but on the approach of a force greatly superior, the captors were reluctantly obliged to relinquish their prize and hasten to the *Otter* with intimation of their disappointment. Every circumstance plainly indicated an intention on the part of the privateer to attack His Majesty's sloop, which immediately got under way, in order to prepare for their reception. While they were weighing, I took leave of the captain and officers and repaired on board the schooner which brought me from Annapolis, in firm expectation that the action would commence before I could possibly proceed far on my return. Shortly after I quitted the *Otter,* she struck on a shoal and heeled considerably, in which situation she could have made very little resistance, had the provincial commander thought it advisable to have then availed himself of that opportunity. She, however, quickly righted, and stood for her opponent who, possibly in pursuance of orders, put about and directed her course for Baltimore. Night approaching and the navigation being intricate, the *Otter* came again to an anchor near the mouth of the Patapsco.

On the ninth, the *Otter* returned down the bay and anchored off the mouth of our harbor, soon after which a flag of truce was dispatched on shore. The officer who brought it was received with respect; two gentlemen of the council of safety were present at the delivery of his message; and the day was concluded at the governor's in a sociable manner. During this interval the seamen who accompanied the officer continued in their boat at a small distance from the shore, where they supported a friendly conversation with the provincial military who were stationed on the beach to preserve regularity.

Early on the ensuing day another flag attended the governor, but continued with him a very short time; and about noon the *Otter* made sail to join the fleet on the Virginia station.

It was certainly a most happy circumstance that this visit was not attended with more serious consequences. Had an action taken place, which at one time appeared too probable, whatever might have been the event, factious and ambitious men would eagerly have embraced the opportunity to have fomented the general discontent. The *Defense,* which is the name of the armed ship fitted out at Baltimore, is much superior in force to the *Otter* sloop, and was crowded with seamen and volunteers, who appeared resolute and determined. Many are of opinion they acted wisely in declining the contest. They had retaken the prize, the avowed object of their intentions; and admitting their claim equal with respect to courage, added to the circumstances of a superior force, these advantages would probably by no means have counterbalanced the acknowledged activity and address which so remarkably distinguishes the seamen of the British navy.

March 25th

I am this day rendered happy by intelligence of your safe arrival and most pleasing reception. Under what a painful, tedious uncertainty have I labored! But my mind is now relieved; you are surrounded by faithful friends who will zealously exert every effort to promote your tranquility. That every wish you form may be speedily and effectually realized will be the constant, ardent prayer of your faithful, etc.

LETTER XXVIII

Annapolis, March 29, 1776

An authentic account arrived this day that the British forces have evacuated Boston, and that General Washington with the continental troops had taken possession. This important event took place on the seventeenth instant. The reasons which rendered this measure necessary will probably reach England at an earlier period than it will reach this part of America. Various opinions are industriously circulated; and some, who pretend to have investigated the real motives of this sudden and unexpected event, consider the conduct of Sir William Howe[1] as a preliminary towards a reconciliation.

The utmost credit is given to the British general for the propriety and regularity with which he conducted the evacuation; and though his design for some days had been manifestly evident, the provincial army continued quiet in their works, without any efforts to obstruct the embarcation or to molest the rear. Several hundreds of the inhabitants, whose attachment to government had rendered them obnoxious, have removed with their families and effects on board the transports and ships of war, and numerous conjectures are formed with respect to their destination. The season of the year operates strongly against a distant voyage. Beacons are therefore established along the coast to give the most immediate notice of their approach, should a design be

---

[1] Sir William Howe (1729-1814) had succeeded General Gage in command at Boston in May 1775.

formed against any other part of the continent which the commanders of His Majesty's forces may deem more accessible. A short time must resolve every doubt.

From present appearances, there are but faint hopes of a speedy reconciliation. Greater requisitions will assuredly be made than, I fear, can consistently be complied with. In political as in moral events, one evil imperceptibly leads to another. The original limited boundary is cast far behind, and new claims and new pursuits are even sanctified by the fallacious plea of justice and necessity. In Maryland a spirit of moderation is yet predominant; and if an opinion may be formed from general appearances, every endeavor is directed to restore a constitutional connection with the parent state. But in several populous and powerful provinces, doctrines are industriously promulgated and eagerly received which will effectually bar every avenue to a pacific accommodation; and the most sanguine adherents to the interests of Great Britain cannot with propriety indulge the faintest idea that any single colony, however influenced by circumstance or inclination, can possibly pretend to stem the torrent should it unhappily tend to the establishment of an independent government.

From such considerations, I am naturally led to believe that the day cannot be far distant when it will be necessary for those to abandon this country who cannot consistently coincide with the popular measures. Be therefore always prepared to see me; and let not my sudden appearance affect your mind too sensibly. On the other hand, yield not to gloomy apprehensions if a considerable time should elapse without your receiving any intimation of my welfare; and be not alarmed when reports are circulated relative to calamities incident to war. Adieu!

LETTER XXIX

Annapolis, May 20, 1776

The Congress by a declaration of the fifteenth instant have earnestly recommended to

the respective assemblies and conventions of the united colonies, where no government sufficient to the exigencies of their affairs has been hitherto established, to adopt such government as shall in the opinion of the representatives of the people best conduce to the happiness and safety of their constituents, and America in general.

This declaration is grounded on the prohibitory act by which "the inhabitants of British America are totally excluded from the protection of the crown." It is also alleged therein

that no answer has been or is like to be returned to the humble petitions of the colonies; but that instead of attending to the redress of grievances, coercive measures are adopted, by which the whole force of the mother country, aided by foreign mercenaries, is to be exerted for their destruction. From such considerations, it is asserted to be absolutely irreconcileable to reason and good conscience to take the oaths and affirmations necessary for the support of any government under the dominion of Great Britain, and therefore expedient that the exercise of every kind of authority under the said crown should be totally suppressed, and all the powers of government hereafter exerted under the authority of the people of the colonies, for the preservation of internal peace, virtue, and good order, as well as for the defense of their lives,

liberties, and properties against the hostile invasions and cruel depredations of their enemies.

Whether any of the provinces, by their delegates in Congress,
have dissented from a measure which must inevitably be
productive of the most serious consequences has not yet
been ascertained; but it is certain that the colony of Virginia
has taken a most decided lead in promoting a total separation from Great Britain. For on the same day in which Congress came to the resolution above-mentioned, the convention in Williamsburg issued a similar declaration, but
expressed in such strong and pointed terms as evidently indicate a settled determination never to acknowledge themselves in any degree subordinate to the influence or authority
of the British government.

There were present that day in convention one hundred
and twelve members who, after stating the reasons which influenced their conduct, conclude with the following *unanimous* resolution.

That the delegates appointed to represent this colony in general
congress be instructed to propose to that respectable body, *to declare the United Colonies free and independent States,* absolved
from all allegiance to, or dependence upon the crown, or parliament of Great Britain; and that they give the assent of this colony
to such declaration, and to whatever measures may be thought
proper and necessary by the Congress for forming foreign alli-
ances, and a confederation of the colonies, at such time, and in
the same manner, as to them shall seem best: PROVIDED, that the
power of forming government for and the regulations of the internal concerns of such colonies be left to the respective colonial
legislatures.

To very many this proceeding appears extraordinary and
premature, commissioners being daily expected to receive
the claims of the colonies in order to adjust and regulate the

terms of reconciliation. It is possible their powers may be ample; surely their extent ought at least to be ascertained previous to any decided measure which may preclude a possibility of entering upon a negotiation. In speaking thus far, I but declare the sentiments of many respectable individuals who have hitherto taken a distinguished lead in opposition to the British legislature; and I most fervently hope that the influence of such men, in the different provinces, will operate with sufficient efficacy to prevent the final declaration of independence until, in their opinion, it becomes an unavoidable expedient and immediately necessary for the interest, the happiness, and the freedom of America.

Friday, May 24

Some events have recently taken place in which I am particularly interested, and which will probably be attended with important consequences to me and mine. But that you may be enabled to form a proper idea of my present critical situation, I must relate some material circumstances which took place early in the preceding month.

A gentleman who had some private concerns with the Earl of Dunmore obtained permission from the council of safety of Maryland to attend His Lordship on board his ship, then lying off the town of Norfolk in Virginia; and on his return he took charge of such letters as were arrived in the fleet, addressed to persons in this province, amongst them was a packet for our governor from Lord George Germain, secretary of state for the American department.

In his passage up the bay he was boarded by an armed vessel in the provincial service, the commander of which examined his papers, and after taking from him the official dispatches, permitted him to proceed to Annapolis with such letters as were totally unconnected with political transactions. On the 6th of April he arrived in this city, by which opportunity I had the happiness to receive your epistle of the sixteenth of November last.

Lord George Germain's letter acknowledged the important information which administration had received from our governor, who was assured "of His Majesty's entire approbation of his conduct, and was directed to proceed in the line of his duty with all possible address and activity."

This packet was forwarded to General Lee, who has the command of the southern district, by whom it was immediately dispatched to Maryland with a strong recommendation to seize the person of the governor, together with all papers and documents of office; by which it was presumed some important discoveries would be made of ministerial intentions.

The council of safety acted on this critical occasion with the utmost moderation and delicacy. Governor Eden, by the affability of his manners and his evident disposition to promote the interests of the province, had conciliated universal regard. They therefore avoided proceeding with that precipitate vigor so strenuously enjoined; and only required him to give his parole, that he would not take any measures for leaving the continent till after the meeting of the next convention.

This requisition the governor for some time warmly resisted; but on conviction that the measure was unavoidable, he thought it necessary to comply; therefore, on the sixteenth of the month, gave every satisfactory assurance.

On the seventh instant the convention assembled, and yesterday they came to a determination respecting my worthy patron; when it was resolved, "that his longer continuance in the province at so critical a period might be prejudicial to the cause in which the colonies were unanimously engaged; and that, therefore, his immediate departure for England was absolutely necessary." An address was accordingly directed to be drawn up and presented to His Excellency, which was delivered to him this evening by a committee of that body.

In this address the sentiments of the convention are expressed in liberal terms: "they acknowledge the services rendered by the governor to the country on many former occasions; and they express the warmest wishes, that when the unhappy disputes which at present prevail are constitutionally accommodated, he may speedily return and reassume the reins of government."

I cannot yet form any conclusion how I am to regulate my conduct on this important occasion. The governor is of opinion that it is my indispensable duty to remain in Maryland, while the ancient form of government is, in any degree, acknowledged and continued. But how long that will be is a matter of great uncertainty.

It is but justice to confess that the most respectable leading men in this province have acted with as much temper and propriety as the nature of the times would admit. Yet I am apprehensive, however favorably they may be now disposed, they will not long be able to stem the torrent which in several provinces runs strongly towards independence. Whatever may be the complexion of my fate, I will continue to act consistently with what I conceive to be my duty; and should necessity compel me to revisit my native clime, I shall assuredly be supported by a consciousness that my misfortunes are derived from inevitable events and not from impropriety of conduct.

Our friends must not expect from my pen any comments on the present operations: I am determined to avoid discussions which cannot possibly answer any salutary purpose; nor will I censure any individual or collective body merely from being actuated by sentiments different from my own. Human nature, even in the full possession of every human acquirement, cannot possibly be exempt from error; and the best intended actions are sometimes liable to censure. I therefore trust it will be ever my disposition to judge in the most favorable manner of my fellow creatures, and acknowledge every man to be right whose conduct is directed by the conscientious dictates of his breast.

Saturday, June 1

Our friend S—— embarked last Sunday for Virginia to learn whether there were any vessels on that station bound for England; and yesterday he returned from his expedition. A ship of war under a flag of truce will shortly be ordered hither to convey the governor down the bay, who is now fully engaged in making preparations for his departure. I am, however, of opinion he will not immediately proceed for Europe, but that he will be anxious to remain near the scene of action until a competent judgment can be formed whether any reconciliation is likely to be effected, an event which a few weeks will probably determine.

Mr. S——, myself, and my colleague are to continue for the present in our respective stations. The first named is charged with the settlement of the governor's private concerns; and as the loan office is of the utmost provincial importance, it is absolutely necessary that the commissioners should continue to act in that department as long as a shadow remains of the ancient constitution. Should those who have now the ascendency think it expedient to model a new system under which I cannot conscientiously remain, I shall avail myself of the first opportunity to take leave of this continent.

In consequence of residing with the governor, I expected an exemption from any penalties inflicted on persons who had refused to associate or enroll. But in this idea I was very materially mistaken. The committee of observation will not consider me as a member of His Excellency's household, alleging in support of their opinion that I hold offices immediately dependent on the province. These are not times to dispute nice points. I have therefore paid ten pounds for my fine and have taken a receipt for the same. My arms have likewise been demanded. I am, however, happy to inform you that I have constantly been treated with kind attention, even by political opponents. It is my endeavor to regulate my conduct with propriety, carefully avoiding mixed company, taking heed that "I offend not with my tongue"; and not permitting my pen to expatiate on the tendency of public transactions. I entrust this to the care of a friend bound to Lisbon; may it safely reach you!

LETTER XXX

Annapolis, June 4, 1776

Every day is pregnant with some new event. I am apprehensive from a recent circumstance that I must quickly bid adieu to Maryland. The committee of observation have this morning served me with a summons to attend them on Thursday next, "to give security for my behavior during the present unhappy contention with Great Britain." I must either comply, submit to imprisonment, or abandon the country. The first I consider as incompatible with my oath of allegiance; confinement is an evil I would most willingly avoid; and a voyage to Europe will inevitably subject me to all the complicated embarrassments attending disappointment and a contracted income; but at all events, I will rely on Providence and persevere in my integrity.

When I appear before the committee, I propose to intimate my intention of returning home, and shall only entreat a reasonable time to adjust my public and private concerns that I may be enabled to leave the province with unsullied reputation. I hope the governor will not sail before my fate is determined.

Friday, June 7

I learn that many of our friends who are supposed to be inimical to the popular cause are also summoned by the committee of observation, so that such consolation as can be derived from having associates in difficulty will at least be afforded me. The concerns of the loan office are of the utmost importance to the public; and some time will be absolutely requisite to adjust them with propriety. The ruling powers will therefore surely be convinced of the necessity of this measure, and comply with a requisition founded on reason and propriety. In that case, a possibility appears that an accommodation may be effected before the expiration of the term which may be allotted for the settlement of that department; and we shall consequently be reinstated with every circumstance of advantage and reputation.

Sunday, June 9

We are in hourly expectation of seeing the ship which is to convey the governor from this province; and though I am solicitous to transmit the result of Tuesday's proceedings, yet on his own account I am anxious for his immediate departure, lest any alteration should take place which may occasion his detention in Maryland.

In my last letter, I mentioned that it was most earnestly recommended by General Lee to seize the person of the governor, together with his papers and official documents. The Congress have also in strong terms urged the expediency of that measure; and the convention of Virginia have likewise come to a similar resolution, which they have published to the world, and which they are endeavoring to enforce with all their power.

The sentiments expressed in the resolve of that province sufficiently evince the danger of delay, as they already appear to operate with great force on the minds of the multitude; and there are some who publicly avow their opinion that the community at large are not bound to yield their assent to any proceedings of delegates, which in their consequences may be prejudicial to the general interests of America.

That you may be enabled to form a clear idea under what embarrassing circumstances the governor is at present situated, I have transcribed the resolve for your more particular information.

IN CONVENTION

Williamsburg, Friday, May 31, 1776

Resolved, *unanimously,* That the committee of safety be directed to write a letter to the President of the Convention of Maryland, in answer to his letter of the twenty-fifth instant, expressing the deepest concern at the proceedings of that Convention, respecting Governor Eden, and our reasons for not becoming accessary thereto, by giving him a passport through this colony or the bay adjoining: that we would with reluctance in any case intermeddle in the affairs of a sister colony, but in this matter we are much interested; and the Convention of Maryland, by sending their proceedings to the committee of safety, have made it the duty of the Convention, to declare their sentiments thereon.

That considering the intercepted letter from Lord George Germaine to Governor Eden, in which his whole conduct and confidential letters are approved, and he is directed to give facility and assistance to the operations of Lord Dunmore against Virginia, we are at a loss to account for the council of safety of Maryland, their having neglected to seize him, according to the recommendation of the general Congress; and more so for the Convention having promoted his passage to assist in our destruction under a pretense of his retiring to England, which we conceive, from the above letter, he is not at liberty to do; that supposing he should go to Britain, it appears to us that such voyage, with the address presented to him, will enable him to assume the character of a public agent, and by promoting division amongst the colonies produce consequences the most fatal to the American cause: that as the reasons assigned for his departure, "That he must obey the ministerial mandates while remaining in his government," are very unsatisfactory, when the Convention declare, that "in his absence the government, in its old form, will devolve on the President of the Council of State," who will be under equal obligation to obey such mandates. We cannot avoid imputing these proceedings to some undue influence of Governor Eden under the mask of friendship to America, and of the proprietary interest in Maryland, whereby the members of that Convention were betrayed into a vote of fatal tendency to the common cause, and, we fear, to this country in particular; and feel it an indispensable duty to warn the good people of that province against the proprietary influence.

Resolved, That the foregoing resolution be forthwith published in the *Virginia Gazette*.

EDM. PENDLETON, *President*
JOHN TAZWELL, *Clk. Convention*

From the above it appears evident that my observations respecting the temper and moderation of those who at present direct the political concernments of this province are well founded. Independence is by no means the general wish in Maryland. Our neighbors are, however, active in propagating the popular doctrines, and I fear the number of proselytes is daily augmenting. The above appeal of the colony of Virginia has already added fuel to the fire; it has increased the zeal of the violent, and may possibly lead to measures which those who are now at the helm have not yet thought it expedient to adopt.

Monday, June 10

Tomorrow I must obey the summons of the Committee. My colleague[1] and I have drawn up the following representation of our case, which we mean to deliver to the chairman of that body in order to obviate the necessity of entering into bond.

[1] John Clapham, associated with Eddis at the provincial loan office.

To the chairman and members of the Committee of Observation for Anne Arundel County.

Gentlemen,

We flatter ourselves that the following representation will engage the Committee's candid and dispassionate consideration; and that when the personal liberty of even an individual is concerned, his endeavors to preserve it will be received with indulgence.

You will please, gentlemen, to observe, that it is not ordered by the Convention, that the Committees of Observation take bonds of all non-associators, but it is left to their discretion whether to require bonds or not; and in the exercise of this power, though the committees are not held as magistrates are in similar cases by the obligation of an oath, yet we presume they are bound in honor not to demand security unnecessary for the public good and inconvenient and embarrassing to the persons called upon.

From the above consideration we inferred, on being required to give up our arms without any demand or hint respecting the entering into bonds, that the Committee of Observation, in their discretion, did not deem it necessary or conducive to the public good. Had we been called upon for that purpose, we should have had an opportunity of appealing immediately to the Convention. To that respectable body we could have represented our peculiar circumstances; that we are officers of the Crown; that we have given security in London for the faithful discharge of our duty, agreeable to instructions from time to time received respecting the revenue of customs; that we are not entitled to our salaries without a nihil account, transmitted quarterly of our proceedings; and that though a correspondence of this nature could be no way injurious to America, yet it might, perhaps, be deemed a breach of the proposed bond, and consequently deprive us of the means of subsistence for ourselves and families; for by the condition of this bond, "no correspondence, directly or indirectly, by letter, message, or otherwise, with any person holding a civil office under the Crown, is allowable," even a demand for, and receipt of, our salaries, would be a breach of the condition prescribed.

Although we are not natives of this country, we are animated with the warmest attachment for its interest and happiness; and we flatter ourselves that our conduct for a term of years has been generally approved, both as servants of the public and members of the community. We are determined to persevere, faithfully and honorably, in discharging the duties of our respective offices as long as with propriety we can act in the same; but we cannot sacrifice our honor or prostitute our oaths for temporary indulgences. Should we be obliged to depart from this continent, we hope we shall be permitted to take leave, with security to our persons and property, agreeably to a resolve of the convention, in that case provided; and wherever we may fix our residence, we shall retain the most affectionate regard for Maryland, without deviating from our allegiance to our sovereign, which has been and will ever continue to be the invariable rule of our conduct.

Not to trespass, gentlemen, upon your time, permit us to assure you that we cannot, consistent with our peace of mind, enter into the proposed bond. We act solely from principle and the dictates of conscience. Relying, therefore, on your impartiality, we shall cheerfully submit to whatever you may please to determine; and however Providence may dispose of us in future, our prayers shall be continually offered for the prosperity of this once happy province, most ardently wishing a permanent and constitutional reconciliation may speedily take place, and that Great Britain and America may remain, to the latest period, one happy, free, and undivided empire.

We are, gentlemen,
Your obedient,
Humble servants,
JOHN CLAPHAM
WM. EDDIS.

Should the committee be pleased to determine, agreeable to the resolve of the Convention, and grant us passes to depart the country, we have only to desire that a sufficient time may be allotted us to settle the various and intricate concerns of the loan office, which we need not observe are of the utmost importance to the community in general. It is also highly incumbent on us to leave the business of that department in a clear state, so that our securities, who are engaged in very large sums for our fidelity, may be honorably discharged from the obligations entered into on our behalf.

We are by no means sanguine with regard to the above application; on the contrary, we are prepared to encounter every disagreeable consequence. It is possible a few weeks may be allotted to adjust provincial and private concerns; we must then give up every flattering expectation, every late erected hope. We must forsake ALL, or act inconsistently with the dictates of honor and of conscience.

The case of my respectable colleague is uncommonly severe. Mrs. Clapham is on the point of adding to a family already numerous and totally dependent on his industry for support. In times like these, it is impossible to dispose of any property in order to raise a sufficiency for their temporary use in England; notwithstanding which, he is determined to encounter the utmost malevolence of fortune, every accumulated evil which penury can inflict, rather than deviate from his principles or violate his allegiance.

Tuesday evening, June 11

We have attended the committee and have heard their decision. On our refusing to enter into bond with good and sufficient security, under the penalty of ten thousand pounds each, we are directed to leave the province before the first of August. I shall be as expeditious as possible in adjusting my concerns and shall probably be with you before the conclusion of September.

Notwithstanding the Convention broke up so lately, they are summoned to meet again in a few days, on account of some important dispatches received from Congress. The Virginians are exceedingly irritated with our ruling powers for permitting the governor to leave the country, and are taking vigorous measures, which they trust will have an effect in this province to his prejudice. All who wish him well are anxious to behold the ship that is to convey him hence, as apprehensions are justly entertained of some violent measures to detain him.

A formidable association has taken place in the town of Baltimore under the appellation of the Whig Club;[2] they loudly proclaim the absolute necessity of seizing and securing the person of the governor as a pledge for the public safety; and it is asserted that a plan is actually in agitation to accomplish this purpose, in defiance of that legislature which themselves have established. Under such a combination of perplexing circumstances, His Excellency conducts himself with the utmost coolness and fortitude; he does not appear to entertain the most remote suspicion, but to rely confidently on the honor of the Convention, which is solemnly pledged for his safe departure.

I mean to entrust this letter to the care of my patron and therefore cannot entertain any apprehension that it will be liable to inspection; and shall, in consequence, venture to make some comments on the late proceedings of the committee of observation.

I believe the demand of such unreasonable security is unprecedented: it is, therefore, evident that the intention of that body is to banish all who are deemed inimical to the popular cause. The case of the crown officers is particularly distressing, as it is well known that they are required, under the most sacred obligations, to give immediate circumstantial information of any designs that may be concerted

---

[2] The Whig Club, self-appointed watchdog of political morals, came to grief in combat with William Goddard over the Tom Tell Truth article in his newspaper. The Club banished Goddard when he claimed the article to be a privileged communication and refused to disclose the name of the author. Goddard left the town, as ordered, but went only as far as Annapolis where he told his story to the convention, which blasted the Club for usurping authority and placed Goddard under its special protection.

against the peace or order of government. Who, therefore, in possession of the least share of reason would consent to hazard so great a penalty on behalf of men who must undoubtedly be guilty of perjury should they neglect an opportunity to convey intelligence? Some of our friends under similar circumstances entertain an opinion that when the Convention meet they will check the authority of the respective committees and afford some indulgence to those who have been unnecessarily oppressed by their power. For my part, I very little rely on such delusive expectations. The utmost moderation and temper, considering the complexion of the times, has indeed hitherto marked the proceedings of that body; but violent and inflammatory men are now industriously straining every nerve to excite general confusion and plunge us fatally deep in schemes of independence. From this powerful consideration I am decidedly of opinion that the Convention will not hazard their influence, or their popularity, by injudiciously attempting to extend any indulgence to a description of men who are too generally proscribed as enemies to the freedom and the interests of America.

The instant the governor embarks I shall establish my temporary residence with my worthy colleague and his family, and with them shall probably bid adieu to Maryland and to a valuable circle of respectable connections.

Sunday, June 16

Not any intelligence is yet received of the expected ship. The governor appears rather anxious for her arrival, and his friends are solicitous for his immediate departure, as there are busy spirits at work who labor to excite commotions with a view to his detention.

It seems to be the general opinion that the colonies will speedily be declared FREE and INDEPENDENT STATES! In that case what dreadful calamities must inevitably ensue! But surely every weighty reason should operate for postponing this most important measure until the commissioners have made known the extent of their powers and the terms they are authorized to propose. Should the colonies be thus precipitate, Great Britain cannot tamely admit the claim, and the sword alone must determine the fatal contest.

Thus circumstanced, I look forward with extreme impatience to the hour of my departure from this country, where every surrounding prospect is dreary and uncomfortable. It is probable I shall be obliged to go by the way of Nova Scotia. From Halifax, the capital of that province, I shall find frequent opportunities of a passage to England; but from this place so few that after I am ready for embarkation I may be detained many weeks before I can be accommodated. But to accomplish my purpose, I must obtain permission to join the British fleet on the Virginia station, from which vessels are frequently dispatched to the general rendezvous.

It is possible that this course may prove advantageous to our private concerns; and I am confident our worthy friend the commissary general will exert his utmost endeavors to render my situation agreeable while I am necessarily detained in that part of America. By the first ship after the receipt of this I request you to inform him that, "as it is probable I shall visit his station previous to my return to Europe, I entreat him to take charge of all letters that may be forwarded to his care." He will gratify his own inclination in rendering us every good office; and on my interview with him I may possibly obtain such information as may enable me to regulate my concerns with a proper attention to our mutual interest.

The convention are to meet on Wednesday, and it is probable, before they rise, that some important measures will be determined on by Congress in which they will be expected to acquiesce. Independence is the general cry of the infatuated multitude; what effects may flow from a proceeding of this nature are dreadful to imagine. Most fervently do I wish the governor safe on board; for though the convention at their former session pledged their honor for his peaceable departure, they may, from an idea of absolute necessity, think themselves justified in rescinding that resolution. The times are so dangerous and unsettled that is is impossible to draw conclusions from present appearances. Every countenance is clouded with suspicion, and the warmest attachments are obliterated by the malignant influence of political contention. The governor apparently continues easy and collected; he is treated with every exterior mark of attention; and I am persuaded the consistency and propriety of his conduct in many trying and peculiar situations will be long remembered with sentiments of esteem and gratitude.

Sunday, June 23

Last night the *Fowey* frigate, commanded by Captain George Montague,[3] arrived off this harbor; and early this morning the first lieutenant came on shore with a flag of truce. The governor will embark in the course of the day. Would he were gone! It is impossible to determine what a minute may produce. The militia are under arms and a general confusion prevails. You can well conceive the sensations I experience on this very affecting occasion.

[3] The *Fowey* and her commander, Captain George Montague, already had a bad reputation. The ship had been Lord Dunmore's floating headquarters when he had to leave Virginia.

LETTER XXXI

Annapolis, June 29, 1776

My last, by the governor, will, I trust, safely reach you; but when an opportunity may again offer to transmit intelligence of my situation is indeed a most painful uncertainty. I shall nevertheless occasionally resume the pen, as circumstances may arise; and as it is my intent carefully to avoid commenting on political transactions, I hope not to encounter any hazard in the course of our future correspondence.

Till the moment of the governor's embarkation on the 23rd, there was every reason to apprehend a change of disposition to his prejudice. Some few were even clamorous for his detention. But the council of safety, who acted under a resolve of the convention, generously ratified the engagements of that body; and after they had taken an affectionate leave of their late supreme magistrate, he was conducted to the barge with every mark of respect due to the elevated station he had so worthily filled.

A few minutes before his departure, I received his strict injunctions to be steady and cautious in the regulation of my conduct, and not to abandon my situation, on any consideration, until absolutely discharged by an authority which might too probably be erected on the ruins of the ancient constitution. I promised the most implicit attention to his salutary advice, and rendered my grateful acknowledgments for the innumerable obligations he had conferred on me; at the same time I offered my most fervent wishes that his future happiness might be in full proportion to the integrity of his conduct and the benevolence of his mind.

In about an hour the barge reached the *Fowey,* and the governor was received on board under a discharge of cannon; his baggage and provisions were left on shore to be forwarded in the course of the ensuing day.

During the night some servants and a soldier belonging to the Maryland regiment found means to escape on board His Majesty's ship, which being almost immediately discovered, a flag was sent off with a message to Captain Montague demanding the restitution of the men previous to any further communication.

Captain Montague in reply acquainted the council of safety "that he could not, consistently with his duty, deliver up any persons who, as subjects of His Britannic Majesty, had fled to him for refuge and protection; that he had strictly given it in charge to such officers as might be sent on shore not to bring off any of the inhabitants without the express permission of the ruling powers; but that the case was extremely different respecting those who had, even at the hazard of life, given evidence of their attachment to the ancient constitution."

This message not being deemed satisfactory, a letter was dispatched to the governor demanding his interference in this critical business, with an intimation that the detention of the men would be considered as a manifest breach of the regulations under which flags of truce are established.

Governor Eden received the officer with proper attention, but replied he had only to observe that on board His Majesty's ship he had not the least authority; and that Captain Montague was not to be influenced by his opinion, as he acted on principles which he conceived to be strictly consistent with the line of his duty.

The event of this negotiation was disagreeable in its conse-

quences to the governor. The populace were exceedingly irritated, and it was thought expedient not only to prohibit
all further intercourse with the *Fowey,* but also to detain
the various stores which the governor had provided for his
voyage to Europe. This resolution was intimated in express
terms; and on the evening of the 24th, Captain Montague
weighed anchor and stood down the bay for his station on
the coast of Virginia.

This incident, inconsiderable as it may appear, will operate strongly against those who have hitherto restrained the
impetuosity of the popular zeal. The delegates in Congress
for this province have been instructed to oppose the declaration of independence; but it now appears almost a general
opinion that Maryland will coincide in every measure which
the uniting colonies may think essential for the interest and
happiness of the general community.

July 2

The 31st of the present month was the extent of time limited for our continuance in Maryland by the committee of
observation in consequence of our refusal to enter into the
proposed bond. Conscious that it was impossible to settle
the concerns of the loan office with satisfaction to the public,
to our securities, and to ourselves, within the term they had
thought proper to prescribe, Mr. Clapham and myself determined to address the convention immediately on their
meeting for such relief as on principles of justice and equity
we were entitled to demand.

We, accordingly, in firm but respectful terms represented
our peculiar circumstances, referring them to the memorial
which had been presented by us to the committee of observation. On due consideration it was agreed by both houses
"to depute some members of their body to investigate the
accounts and transactions of the commissioners of the loan

office, to discharge them from that important trust, and to appoint others to succeed them therein."

In consequence of this determination, a considerable period may possibly elapse before this business will be finally adjusted, till which time we shall be permitted to remain quietly in the country without any further requisition to enter into engagements. This undoubtedly is a great point gained in our favor, procrastination being with us an object of the utmost importance. A short time may be productive of events conducive to public and private tranquility. "Hope springs eternal." But were a judgment to be formed from the present aspect of political concerns, every peaceful expectation must be abandoned.

Annapolis, July 8

At length the decisive blow is struck. The colonies, by their delegates in congress, are declared Free and Independent States, which great event took place on the fourth instant! By this act they have abjured all allegiance to the British crown; and have renounced every political connection with the land from which they derive their origin. The declaration will soon reach England and will be found to contain a long catalogue of grievances. This composition, which is replete with invective, is not more temperate than the measures which it professes to defend. What effect it will have on the councils and operations of government a short time will possibly determine.

I cannot but contemplate with horror the complicated miseries which appear ready to overwhelm this devoted country. Thousands who at this instant are flushed with hope and exulting in a total separation from the interests of the parent state, will probably, before many months elapse, execrate the precipitation by which they have been hurried into measures fatally prejudicial to their repose and happiness.

Before you receive this, the particulars of the action off Charleston in South Carolina on the 28th of June will be in the possession of government. Our accounts say the British troops were totally defeated with a prodigious loss, after many exertions perfectly characteristic of the national bravery. It is reported that the quarter deck of the *Bristol* was, at one time, cleared of every person but the intrepid Sir Peter Parker, who stood alone, a spectacle of heroic firmness never exceeded in military history. Three of the English frigates, by accident or through the ignorance of their pilot, were entangled in some shoals, where for a long time they appeared to be immovably fixed. With great damage and difficulty, two were at length got off, but not in a condition to render any effectual service. The *Acteon,* of twenty-eight guns, was burnt by her officers and crew on the following morning to prevent her falling into the hands of the provincials, every effort having proved ineffectual to remove her from her situation. This decisive victory, as it is here termed, has given great spirits to the advocates for the new government, and will tend to confirm them in their hostile disposition.

I trust this to a circuitous passage. It will be forwarded by the French islands. Entertain not the most distant apprehension with respect to my safety; I am treated with liberality and attention. When shall I again acknowledge a letter from you? To remain thus ignorant of the situation of my family is a weighty addition to the complicated evils I encounter. We must submit with fortitude!

LETTER XXXII

Annapolis, August 1, 1776

On the 14th ultimo Lord Howe[1] safely arrived at Staten Island, after having been long expected by many persons with the most anxious impatience.

His Lordship immediately dispatched on shore by a flag a circular letter to the governors of the colonies, acquainting them with the powers with which he was invested, and desiring that they would publish, as generally as possible, an enclosed declaration of the British legislature.

In this declaration the public are acquainted with the powers himself and his brother, the general, are invested with, under the late act of parliament, by which they are authorized

To grant general or particular pardons to those who, in the tumult of the times, might have deviated from their just allegiance; and who were willing, by a speedy return to their duty, to reap the benefits of the royal favour. . . . The commissioners have likewise the power of declaring any colony, town, or district, to be at His Majesty's peace; in which case the penal provisions of that law would cease in their favor. A due consideration is likewise promised to the services of all persons who may contribute to the restoration of the public tranquility.

---

[1] Admiral Richard Howe (1726-1799) commanded British naval forces on the American station. The crown had joined his brother, Sir William Howe, with him in a commission to treat with the colonists.

The above papers having been immediately forwarded by General Washington to Congress, were as speedily published by their directions in all the prints throughout the united colonies, accompanied with the following resolution.

IN CONGRESS

July 19

RESOLVED, that a copy of the circular letters and of the declaration they enclosed from Lord Howe, to Mr. Franklin, Mr. Eden, Lord Dunmore, Mr. Martin, and Sir James Wright, late governors, sent to Amboy by a flag and forwarded to Congress by General Washington, be published in the several gazettes, that the good people of these United States may be informed of what *nature* are the commissions, and what the *terms,* with the expectation of which the insidious court of Great Britain has endeavored to amuse and disarm them: and that the few who still remain suspended by a hope founded either in the justice or moderation of their late King may now, at length, be convinced that the valor alone of their country is to save its liberties.

CHARLES TOMSON,[2] Sec.

Thus are the sanguine expectations of multitudes cruelly frustrated, it being esteemed criminal by the ruling powers to assert the pacific inclinations of the British ministry. On the contrary, it is loudly maintained that unconditional submission is the only ground on which the commissioners are empowered to treat, and therefore to commence any negotiation on such a basis would be inconsistent with good sense, sound policy, and the essential interests of America. "All hope excluded thus," we must prepare for consequences of the most serious nature, not the most distant probability appearing of a friendly accommodation.

---

[2] Charles Tomson, Pennsylvania radical leader, was from 1774 until 1789 secretary of the Continental Congress.

August 9

Advice is received that Lord Dunmore with his fleet has quitted the coast of Virginia, and is supposed to be gone to the southward. By every account, the hardships experienced by the loyalists and by all who were on board those ships have been dreadful in the extreme. The intense heat of the weather, the badness and scarcity of water and provisions, together with the closeness of the small vessels in which the wretched fugitives were crowded, produced a malignant fever, which made great havoc, but more particularly affected the negroes, most of whom were carried off by the violence of the disorder. Thus are the hopes terminated with respect to the emancipation of slaves in order to suppress the commotions in the southern colonies.

Thursday, September 5

Intelligence of a most alarming nature has been transmitted from New York. On the twenty-second ultimo, the British forces landed without opposition near Utrecht and Gravesend, on the southwest end of Long Island; and on the twenty-seventh a desperate action ensued, which has proved fatal to the arms of America.[3] Particulars of the loss in killed, wounded, and prisoners are not yet ascertained. Maryland has suffered most severely in this conflict, many young men of the most respectable families being included in the number of the slain. General Washington has effected a masterly retreat with the residue of the provincial army to New York, which is represented as invulnerable. This defeat does not yet appear to be attended with such consequences as might naturally be expected; the colonists seem to depend on their internal resources, and defy the utmost exertions of

[3] Eddis refers to the operation, not fatal but certainly disastrous, now known as the Battle of Long Island or the Battle of Brooklyn.

a brave and conquering enemy. There are, however, moderate men, and some of considerable influence, who are inclined to think that the late event may induce the leaders in Congress to commence an immediate negotiation with the parliamentary commissioners. Whatever may tend to the restoration of peace cannot but afford the highest gratification to every humane, benevolent mind.

Monday, September 16

In consequence of a message sent by Lord Howe to Congress, three gentlemen were deputed to confer with him and the general, in order to learn the extent of their authority and to hear such propositions as they were enabled to make.

Dr. Franklin, Mr. Adams, and Mr. Rutledge[4] were the committee appointed on this very interesting occasion; and the report they have made to Congress on the subject of their conference has totally destroyed every pleasing idea of a pacific treaty.

The following are the words in which the committee have thought proper to sum up the particulars of their late negotiation; and I shall only add on the subject that reasons are from this deduced to prosecute the war with the utmost vigor against the power and authority of the mother country.

Upon the whole, it did not appear to your committee that His Lordship's commission contained any other authority of importance than what is contained in the act of Parliament, viz., that of granting pardons, with such exceptions as the commissioners shall think proper to make, and of declaring America, or any part of it, to be in the King's peace upon submission: for as to the power of

[4] Benjamin Franklin, John Adams, and Edward Rutledge met with the Howe brothers at Billopp House on Staten Island in what proved a fruitless conference.

inquiring into the state of America, which His Lordship mentioned to us, and of conferring and consulting with any persons the commissioners might think proper; and representing the result of such conversations to the ministry, who (provided the colonies would subject themselves) might, after all, or might not, at their pleasure, make any alterations in the former instructions to governors, or propose in parliament any amendment of the acts complained of, we apprehend any expectation from the effect of such a power would have been too uncertain and precarious to be relied on by America, had she still continued in her state of dependence.

Tuesday, September 24

The city of New York is in the possession of Sir William Howe; but the provincials have still great strength in the vicinity of that capital, and talk of maintaining their ground till reinforcements arrive, which may enable them to retrieve with effect every past calamity. This event happened on the fifteenth instant, and we are hourly in expectation of further important transactions.

Tuesday, October 1

Though the declaration of independence was made on the fourth of July last, the form of government with respect to Maryland is by no means finally adjusted; and from the delay which has been evident in the proceedings of our Convention and the committees subordinate to their direction, I cannot but indulge the pleasing idea, in spite of hostile operations, that the moderate and dispassionate who are included in those bodies have still sufficient influence to retard an absolute establishment of the new constitution; while the most distant possibility remains of a reconciliation being effected.

The committee appointed to investigate the accounts of the loan office also appear dilatory in bringing the affairs of that department to a conclusion; and you very well know how particularly I am engaged, both in honor and gratitude, to obtain an ample and proper discharge from an employment of so much importance to the community.

From the present political appearances I cannot but indulge an opinion that our legislative body will not proceed with alacrity in the prosecution of this business. A short, a very short time, will probably determine how far the colonies are enabled to support coercive measures against the formidable exertions of the British nation; and should the least prospect appear of returning peace, it would be impolitic and fruitless to discharge officers who would immediately be reinstated with advantage on affairs reverting into the ancient channel.

My worthy colleague and his family are preparing to remove from Annapolis to a house belonging to Mr. Dulany on Hunting Ridge, about six miles distant from Baltimore, to which place I intend to accompany them. We propose to attend alternately in this city until discharged from our employments or confirmed in them.

Hunting Ridge, November 1

I write to you from one of the most delightful situations on the continent of America, where I have obtained an occasional retreat from the noise, the tumult, and the miseries of the public world. From the back piazza of our habitation we command a truly picturesque view into several fertile counties; a distant prospect of the eastern shore; the magnificent waters of the Chesapeake, and the river Patapsco, from the entrance at the Bodkin Point to its apparent termination at the town of Baltimore. After this inadequate description, I need not observe that we reside on a lofty eminence where

—— the air
Nimbly, and sweetly recommends itself
Unto our gentle senses.

As Mr. Clapham and myself are not yet superseded in our office, we attend in rotation, every other week, in Annapolis, from which this place is about thirty miles distant. The contrast we experience on these occasions is hardly to be described, from the churlish sounds of hostile preparation to the calm enjoyments of peaceful retirement. Though in the vicinity of a large and populous town agitated with uproar and confusion and rumors of approaching calamities, here, sheltered by surrounding woods, we are entirely secluded "from the busy haunts of men," and are benevolently permitted to enjoy our retirement without dread of molestation. It is well known that we have never attempted by any injudicious steps to incur the resentment of those who conceive they are warranted by justice and by duty to take a contrary part; and while we thus continue to regulate our conduct, we shall surely experience attention with the most perfect security.

Hunting Ridge, December 1

The whole of York Island is in the possession of His Majesty's forces. General Howe has for some time been attempting to force General Washington to a decisive action, which he has hitherto avoided with the penetration of a Fabius. Sir William, finding every well-concerted effort ineffectual to accomplish this purpose, has directed his arms against the garrison left for the defense of Fort Washington, a very strong post situated on a lofty eminence and to which the approaches were extremely difficult.

On the thirteenth of November, the provincial commander was summoned to surrender, which he rufused to do in the most peremptory terms, declaring he would defend his station to the last extremity. A general assault was, in consequence, determined upon, which took place on the sixteenth, when the fort was carried after a spirited defense; and the garrison, consisting of near three thousand men, became prisoners of war.

On the eighteenth, Lord Cornwallis[5] with a strong detachment passed the North River in order to attack Fort Lee and to make some impression in the Jerseys, in which undertaking he was so successful that the garrison, consisting of about two thousand men, had a very narrow escape by abandoning the post immediately before His Lordship's arrival, leaving their artillery, stores, and tents behind them.

For the particulars of these important transactions I shall refer you to the accounts transmitted home to administration; and have only to offer my most fervent prayers that the rapid successes which have hitherto attended the British arms may be productive of an honorable and permanent reconciliation, founded on such principles as may secure to America the inestimable blessings of liberty, with every consequence attending an abundant population and an extensive commerce.

I fear many of my letters will miscarry; but I hazard every opportunity of writing. I am persuaded you do the same, though fortune has hitherto been adverse to my wishes. Oppose with all your power the intrusion of anxious thoughts, and believe me unalterably yours.

[5] Charles, second Earl Cornwallis (1738-1805), a major general, served under Sir William Howe and his successor, Sir Henry Clinton.

LETTER XXXIII

Annapolis, January 1, 1777

Since the day our hearts and interests were united, frequent occasions have been afforded for the exercise of our fortitude and resignation, and by the blessing of Heaven we have hitherto been safely conducted through every vicissitude. Let us then take courage from past experience. The year opens with the most dreary prospects. The recent event of Trenton will add strength to the sinews of war and cruelly procrastinate the wished return of peace.[1]

The capture of Rhode Island, which happened on the eighth of December, and the surprising of General Lee on the thirteenth by Colonel Harcourt, were circumstances which excited sanguine hopes in the breasts of those who persevered in their attachment to the ancient constitution; and these hopes were encouraged by a strong probability that Philadelphia must speedily follow the fortune of New York, the Delaware being the only apparent obstacle that seemed likely to oppose the progress of the royal arms.

The provincial forces, who were only enlisted for a stipulated time, discouraged by a succession of unfavorable events, were so greatly reduced in their numbers, that it is asserted, on the day preceding the affair at Trenton, the muster roll scarcely exceeded three thousand men; and the greater part of those were anxious for the expiration of their term that they might return to their families and their accustomed vo-

[1] Eddis refers here to Washington's surprise and capture of the Hessians at Trenton on December 26, 1776.

cations. The Congress, from a well founded apprehension of danger, retreated with precipitation to Baltimore;[2] and many who had been most zealous in promoting hostile measures began to avow sentiments of a conciliatory nature; in a word, the general disposition of the colonies tended to a reconciliation, and even the submission of some of the provinces was daily expected.

Affairs were in this promising train when the American general planned and executed the late important enterprise. Trifling as this maneuver might have been considered in the prosecution of a regular war, it has been in this instance attended with the most prejudicial and alarming consequences to His Majesty's arms. It has given spirits to those who showed the utmost despondency; it has recruited the enfeebled ranks; and it has enabled the enthusiastic leaders to magnify in the most exaggerated terms the advantages that must inevitably arise from the success of this brilliant exertion.

To many it has appeared extraordinary that the advanced post was occupied by Hessian regiments who might reasonably be supposed less competent than British to determine on the authenticity of intelligence or the disposition of the colonists with respect to political attachment. But how far censure is well founded, it becomes not an individual to determine. It ought rather to be concluded that those arrangements took place which, on mature reflection, apparently led to the advance of the general service.

The mode hitherto adopted by Congress in conducting their enlistments has been found so inadequate to every essential purpose that they have concluded on adopting a different one, which affords the probability of a permanent army under the most strict and regular military discipline. Hitherto their troops have been raised with a condition of

[2] Congress had fled Philadelphia in mid-December and met in Baltimore until the end of February 1777.

receiving their discharge at the expiration of twelve months; and they conceived that this rotation of duty would occasion the weight to fall less heavy on the general community. But such a continual succession of men, unexperienced and impatient of restraint, has rather impeded than promoted the success of their operations. It is therefore resolved to prosecute the new levies on a settled establishment. Those who engage to enlist during the continuance of the war are to have an immediate bounty of twenty dollars; and one hundred acres of land each at the expiration of their service. Officers are to be rewarded in proportion to their respective situations. Others are admitted for the stipulated term of three years who are to receive the same bounty without any landed compensation. By this regulation it is supposed a very formidable army will be ready to take the field early in the ensuing spring, under a commander who has inspired every adherent to the measures of Congress with the most unlimited confidence in his superior abilities.

It is confidently asserted, and it appears to be universally believed, that General Washington will quickly be enabled to repossess the Jerseys, and to contract the British posts into a very limited sphere of action. This is certain, that apprehensions respecting Philadelphia are no longer seriously entertained, Congress having it in contemplation speedily to resume their deliberations in that city.

Myself and colleague are not yet superseded in our provincial employment, but the day is assuredly at hand. When that event has taken place, I am persuaded I shall be at liberty to revisit England, and have reason to believe I shall be necessitated to shape my course by way of the West Indies. I think it possible we may be restored to each other early in the ensuing summer.

It has been a matter of surprise to many that the capes of Virginia have, in a great measure, been left open since the departure of Lord Dunmore and his fleet from the Chesapeake. In consequence of this apparent remissness on the part of the British cruisers, a considerable commerce is carried on with very little interruption between Virginia and Maryland and the French and Dutch islands, and even with several ports on the continent of Europe. Those who continue attached to the interest of Britain behold with infinite concern many valuable prizes continually brought into American harbors by privateers so inconsiderable in appearance that they might readily be mistaken for boats belonging to the vessels they were triumphantly conducting. Almost all the ships which have hitherto been taken had not the least apprehension of danger, consequently were not prepared for resistance; and if a certain judgment may be formed from the success which has attended the adventurers from this and the adjacent colony, Great Britain must sensibly experience the loss she has already sustained, by the rapid and spirited exertions, which have been so unexpectedly directed against her commerce.

The exorbitant price of almost every essential article exceeds credibility. Those few who are in possession of specie do not permit it to circulate; and the constant depreciation of the paper currency baffles every attempt of the legislature to support its credit; yet in spite of every apparently insurmountable obstacle, the utmost alacrity appears for the prosecution of the war; and the most sanguine hopes are evidently entertained that the political connection between Great Britain and America is finally and effectually dissolved.

The internal government of Maryland is not yet perfectly adjusted, but the arrangements under the new constitution are in great forwardness, and will speedily take place in the various departments. Our discharge will undoubtedly immediately follow, and we shall be free to shape our course as Providence may direct.

When we again meet, I trust we shall find friends, "though

they grow not thick on every bough," who will promote our endeavors to obtain a competent maintenance. Under all the varied circumstances of life we will steadily labor to merit success; and should our best endeavors be frustrated, we shall at least be exempt from self accusation, and can derive no little satisfaction from a consciousness that our sufferings are not the bitter fruits of dissipation or misconduct.

Frederick County, March 1, 1777

Change of scene is frequently conducive to a temporary tranquility. In order therefore to obtain, if possible, some relief, some mitigation of my anxiety, I set out, about twelve days since, on a visiting excursion into this fertile and beautiful country; and am now beneath the hospitable roof of Dr. John Stephenson in the vicinity of Frederick Town, where I have been entertained with that genuine hospitality which so remarkably characterizes the *American Romulus.**

On my return to the Ridge, I expect some material information relative to my particular situation; and have reason to believe that I am, before this, reduced to a private station, and that one journey to Annapolis will settle my concerns as an officer under the ancient constitution; after which I shall certainly embrace the earliest opportunity of departing from the wretched scene of confusion which this country at present exhibits.

Hunting Ridge, April 2

We are at length superseded in our department as commissioners of the loan office; but it is probable some time will elapse before we shall obtain our final discharge, as the ac-

* See page 50.

counts and transactions must undergo the investigation of a committee of both houses. I shall be extremely impatient for the conclusion of this business; after which I cannot entertain a doubt of procuring an immediate passport from America.

On the twenty-first of last month, a letter arrived from Sir Robert Eden, whose integrity and services have procured him an honorable distinction. A prelude, let us hope, to more essential advantages.

On the same day which brought the above pleasing intelligence, Mr. Thomas Johnson[1] was proclaimed governor of of the state of Maryland; the cannon from the ramparts were discharged at the conclusion of the ceremony; the military were under arms, and the American standard was hoisted on the principal battery.

Every circumstance tends to convince me that I must quickly bid farewell to a country where I have experienced many benefits and formed many valuable connections. Could I obtain permission to visit New York in my way to Europe, I am certain I should there meet with letters of the greatest importance to my interest and happiness. Influenced by that consideration, I have applied for the necessary passport to be granted immediately after the affairs of the loan office are finally adjusted. I cannot say that I entertain any great hopes of success; and most of my friends are of opinion I shall meet a refusal; in which case I must be content with a circuitous and expensive passage by way of the West Indies. Reduced as I am in my circumstances, how I am to raise the necessary supply is a very serious consideration; but I will not agitate my mind with the concerns of a future day. It is a proof of imbecility to "shape the fashion of uncertain evils."

[1] Thomas Johnson (1732-1819), a member of the Continental Congress, was elected first governor of Maryland under the new constitution in 1777.

April 12

My application for permission to enter the British lines is positively rejected; I must therefore be content to take my passage by way of the French islands.

Annapolis, May 1

I have taken my leave of Hunting Ridge, and trust I am on the point of bidding farewell to Maryland. The concerns of the loan office will, I hope, be adjusted in a few days; I have agreed for my passage in a vessel bound from Alexandria in Virginia to Martinique, from which place I shall pursue the path which Providence may direct.

Annapolis, June 1

The affairs of the loan office were closed but yesterday, when my colleague and myself obtained a most ample and honorable discharge from that employment.

The ship I proposed sailing in is yet at Alexandria, but her destination is changed, she being ordered to Bordeaux and her departure uncertain.

Mr. Dulany, who was to have participated in my fortune, has taken his passage in an armed schooner, which in my circumstances I do not conceive to be an eligible method; I shall therefore leave him to his chance and pursue myself another course.

Mr. Clapham sets out this day for his delectable retirement on Hunting Ridge. When shall we meet again? I most fervently hope he will be permitted to enjoy his humble retreat without fear of molestation; at all events he must be greatly embarrassed to support his numerous family with any degree of comfort. Indeed he will have full occasion for the exertion of his utmost fortitude; but his established character, and his manly, generous disposition must secure to him attention and respect under every change of fortune.

Wednesday, June 4

Yesterday I received my passport, and wait only the arrival of the post on Friday to determine my course. I have written to my friend Mr. C[arroll],[2] who is a member of Congress, on the subject of obtaining permission to enter the British lines; and have represented in the strongest terms I was able,

the peculiarity of my situation, and my total incapacity to support the heavy additional expense which must attend a voyage to Europe by way of the Islands; I have also urged domestic motives; in short, I have suggested every reason which can induce compliance; I have even requested to be considered as a prisoner upon parole, and have offered to remain in Philadelphia, or in some American post, until I can, by application to my friends in New York, obtain some person in a civil capacity to be exchanged for me.

Should I succeed in this attempt, it is possible I may be relieved in a few days from a state of inexpressible anxiety by receiving intelligence respecting those who occupy every thought, and whose interest and happiness are the primary objects of my attention. If I fail, I must submit to the disappointment with fortitude, supported by the reflection that I have directed my best efforts to the accomplishment of my wishes; and that the failure has not proceeded from any neglect on my part or any impropriety of conduct. At all events, on Saturday or Sunday I shall set out for Philadelphia, or cross the Chesapeake, and proceed to an inlet on the eastern

[2] Charles Carroll of Carrollton (1737-1832), signer of the Declaration of Independence, then just beginning his political career serving in the Continental Congress.

shore, from which I am informed there are frequent opportunities of passing to the French islands.

I mentioned that we had obtained a most honorable discharge from our late provincial department; as I am well convinced it will be highly pleasing to you to learn any circumstance which reflects credit on my reputation, I give you the following extract from the report to both houses.

Your committee further take leave to report that, from the multiplicity of business, the nature of the trust, and the care and regularity of the transactions, they are of opinion that the commissioners' and clerks' annual salaries have been very inadequate to the services they have rendered the public.

Mr. Dulany is in hourly expectation of the armed vessel in which he has taken his passage for France; I mean to entrust this packet to his care, and should he be detained till Friday evening I shall be able to inform you particularly what route I intend to pursue.

General Washington is said to be in great force, and in possession of a strong country in the vicinity of Brunswick; it is therefore probable that some important event will speedily happen which may bring this fatal contest to a decisive issue. It seems, however, to be a prevailing opinion that Sir William Howe will find great difficulty in forcing his wary opponent to a general action, unless obvious advantages justify the measure.

Friday Evening, June 6

My fate is determined. Reasonable as my requisition appeared, it cannot possibly be complied with; I must therefore embrace the only means afforded me, under a perfect conviction of this great truth, that "Whatever is, is right."

Saturday Morning, June 7

A more certain method offers than by way of the eastern shore. So far I appear successful. Last night a vessel arrived off Annapolis, bound to Cape François in Hispaniola, from whence to Jamaica the distance is not considerable. I have agreed with the master for my passage, and tomorrow we are to sail for our destined port.

How strange are the events of human life! I am now preparing to revisit the town of Kingston, where I shall possibly meet some ancient friends for whom I still cherish a grateful attachment.

Saturday Evening

I have taken leave of the few faithful friends still residing in Annapolis. Perhaps a final one! It is a painful distressing idea! But I am hastening to those, my separation from whom I have so long felt and lamented. That thought will firmly support me under every anxious trial it may be yet my fortune to encounter. I shall embark in a few minutes. So will Mr. Dulany, as his vessel is likewise in the harbor and ready for sea. Our projected route, though aiming at the same point, is widely different. I shall deliver this to his care. Should he accomplish his passage agreeable to his wishes, he must reach England long before I can possibly expect that happiness. Adieu!

LETTER XXXV

On board his Majesty's Ship Emerald,
Cape of Virginia, July 2, 1777

After encountering a variety of perplexing and vexatious circumstances, I have met with success beyond my most sanguine expectations. The most agreeable prospects are opening to my view; and I shall speedily obtain ample compensation for those various anxieties which have so long disturbed my repose.

My last intimated that I had taken my passage from Maryland in a vessel bound to Cape François in the island of Hispaniola. On the evening of the seventh of June I took an affectionate leave of our few Annapolitan friends; and, I need not say, such were my sensations on the occasion that I repaired on board the ship destined to convey me from that province with a mind greatly distressed and agitated.

It would have evinced the utmost insensibility to have quitted, without such feelings the scene of former happiness and prosperity. I reflected on the obligations we had received, the benefits we had experienced, and the connections we had formed. I could not resist the united impressions excited by such interesting ideas; nor did I quit my pensive station on the deck while a single object could be distinguished that so forcibly reminded me of past felicity.

Soon as the day dawned on the eighth we weighed anchor and stood down the bay with a propitious gale. I found two gentlemen on board, proprietors of the vessel and cargo; knowing them well, I promised myself great satisfaction from their society and my expectations were completely gratified.

As we passed the mouth of Patuxent, I beheld with emotions of gratitude the hospitable mansion of our benevolent friend. Those doors which ever opened with equal alacrity to the weary traveler and to the opulent guest are now forsaken, even by the generous worthy owner! The colonel, his lady, and family are retired into the interior country, that they may be further removed from the inevitable calamities of war.

Our passage down the bay was tedious, the winds proving variable. On Saturday the 14th, when we were standing in for York River in order to obtain information and to avail ourselves of a proper opportunity to prosecute our course, we descried a British ship in chase of an American sloop. My sensations on this occasion were such as I cannot possibly delineate; and I could scarce refrain expressing a wish that the English colors were flying on our ensign staff. The master of our vessel and my fellow passengers were for some time apprehensive of danger; and I believe we were greatly indebted for our escape to some considerable shoals, which rendered the navigation extremely intricate and dangerous. Our captain, being an expert seaman, profited by the advantages he possessed; and in a short time we were safely at an anchor opposite to the town of York and close beneath the stern of an American frigate.

My companions, though well inclined to government, expressed much satisfaction on finding themselves secure within the limits of an American port, for had they been captured, notwithstanding their sentiments were loyal, their property would have been justly forfeited, as they were attempting to support an illicit commerce. To this measure they were, however, reduced by absolute necessity; it was the only means they could possibly devise to quit their wretched country without embarrassing their friends and relatives, who were compelled by unavoidable circumstances to continue in the province.

These gentlemen finding the capes effectually guarded by several of His Majesty's ships, and being consequently convinced that it was impracticable to pass them with any degree of safety, determined to remain in Virginia until a more favorable opportunity presented itself. This determination by no means accorded with my wishes. The least detention appeared hostile to my happiness; and under my peculiar circumstances, if no motives of a superior nature had operated, I could not support without the greatest inconvenience the accumulated expense which unavoidably must have attended such a measure. I therefore began to devise some proper method of abandoning a situation which threatened a tedious and painful obstruction to the renewal of our domestic intercourse.

Animated by such considerations, I resolved on an immediate application to the officer who commanded the provincial troops in that district. To this gentleman I explained my particular situation, without the least reserve: the pressing motives which required my immediate presence in England, the disappointment I had sustained by the detention of our vessel, and the advantages which would arise to me by a permission to be put on board one of the British cruisers, from whence by way of New York I might obtain a speedy conveyance to my family and connections in Europe. To corroborate assertions founded on the strictest truth, I submitted to his consideration the passport which had been granted to me by the ruling powers in Maryland.

I was heard by this officer with candid attention, and the propriety of my plea was readily admitted; he could not conceive the necessity of waiting a distant opportunity or of prosecuting my voyage by way of the West Indies, therefore advised me to proceed immediately to Hampton where some Virginian gentlemen, adherents to the former government, were on the point of embarking for New York under the operation of an act of their legislature; and he was persuaded, on an explicit representation of my case, I should not find any difficulty in being permitted to avail myself of the benefit of the flag, under the protection of which those persons were preparing to quit the colony.

You will admit that I dispatched this important concern with becoming spirit and expedition, for on Monday the 16th I exchanged reciprocal wishes with my Maryland friends and left them to pursue fortune agreeably to the mode they had adopted.

About noon, the weather being intensely hot, I embarked in a small open boat for the place of my destination, which was about ten leagues nearer to the sea. The capes opened to our view a considerable time before we obtained sight of Hampton, and I anticipated the happiness I expected shortly to experience by passing them on a more eligible plan than necessity had originally suggested. I fondly conceived that I had almost surmounted every difficulty, and could not avoid congratulating myself on the happy address by which I had so fortunately converted an apparent disappointment into such real advantage. Supported by these ideas, I experienced but little inconvenience during several hours that I was confined in a very limited and exposed situation; and scarcely had I reached my desired harbor where a new scene of operations was to commence before a tremendous gale arose, which raged for several hours with incredible violence and threatened inevitable destruction to those who were exposed to its fury. Perhaps I was wrong, but I could not avoid drawing the most favorable conclusions from this dreadful elementary war. I considered my escape as an undoubted prelude to future prosperity, and I experienced a confidence in my mind which led me boldly forward to the completion of my arduous design. But scarce had I landed on the beach ere I experienced a disappointment which overthrew all my late hopes. Those gentlemen in whose fortune I trusted to have participated and for which purpose I had trained my utmost abilities and hazarded the most imminent danger, were embarked the preceding evening, and left melancholy impressions on the minds of their friends on account of the sudden, and violent tempest.*

How to extricate myself from the difficulties which now surrounded me I knew not. I was in a place where I had not the slightest connection, and where the appearance of a stranger was a sufficient motive to excite suspicion. Time, however, was precious; I therefore determined not to lose a moment. It was generally known in Maryland that I had taken my passage by way of the islands; and it was possible I might meet some person from that province who would throw insurmountable obstacles in my way by representing my intentions in an unfavorable point of view. Agitated by such apprehensions and encouraged by the success which had attended my application at Yorktown, I waited instantly on the commanding officer, and assuming a confidence necessary in my situation, intimated the circumstances of my disappointment by the necessity of taking shelter in York River, the motives which had brought me to that place in consequence of it, and the inexpressible mortification I had experienced by arriving too late to avail myself of so favorable an opportunity. I therefore entreated that he would facilitate a reunion with my family and connections by granting me the indulgence of a flag under the conduct of which I might obtain a temporary situation on board one of the British ships stationed in the vicinity of the capes, until an opportunity offered to convey me to some port from whence I might find a ready passage to England.

From the commencement of the war I had established it as a fixed principle that they who were actually engaged in

* The author had the satisfaction to learn, on his arrival at New York, that they had safely accomplished their passage.

hostile opposition were directed by more liberal sentiments than those inflammatory demagogues who had arisen to eminence by fomenting discontents and taking a distinguished lead in popular assemblies; and experience, on various occasions, has fully confirmed the truth of this observation.

In Hampton, fortunately for me, all public affairs were under military direction; the person who commanded attended with complacency to my application, and expressed an earnest solicitude to render me every possible service consistent with his duty.

On the following day (the 17th) this business was more fully investigated in presence of the officer who directed the marine department; and on my delivering the passport which had been granted for my departure from Maryland, no reasons appeared to operate against compliance with my request; therefore to my inexpressible joy, leave was immediately granted to engage a vessel for my passage, and a gentleman was deputed to attend me with a flag as soon as I gave intimation that I was ready for my departure.

Favorable as appearances now were, it was my fate still to encounter disappointment. I found infinite difficulty in procuring a boat, from a settled persuasion that notwithstanding a flag was granted, it was dangerous to rely on that privilege. Every hour's delay increased my disquietude; yet it was not until about noon on the 20th that I was able to accomplish my purpose.

When the necessary arrangements for our departure were made, I rendered my grateful acknowledgments where they were so justly due, and accompanied by the officer who was appointed to conduct me, repaired to the landing place where a vessel was waiting for our reception. Unfortunately at that critical period the wind freshened to a perfect gale, the sea run high, and my companion, from an apprehension of danger, intimated his resolution to postpone the undertaking till the weather was more moderate. It was in vain that I urged every motive to alter his determination; my best arguments were ineffectual; and, with inexpressible reluctance I was obliged to relinquish my design and wait the event of the ensuing day.

Anxious with respect to the great concern which occupied my mind, a short time before sunset I repaired to the harbor to gain information relative to the state of the weather and the probable time when it might be advisable to resume our undertaking. The person whose schooner I had engaged comforted me with the most favorable intelligence, and advised me to be on board by the dawn of day, that advantage might be derived from the land breeze which generally prevailed at that season of the year till the sun had attained a considerable height above the horizon. With alacrity I hastened to communicate these particulars to the officer who had been appointed to attend me when I received intelligence which disconcerted every plan and presented to my dejected view a gloomy prospect of insurmountable difficulties. In short, he informed me that the battalion then quartered in Hampton had that instant received orders to march, early on the following morning, to join the grand army under command of General Washington; and that consequently he could not gratify his own feelings by forwarding my intentions of quitting America.

This intimation, so sudden, so unexpected, affected my mind in the most sensible manner. The officer to whom I had delivered my passport had already taken his departure, and though I could obtain evidence that I had been in possession of such a credential, yet I might have to negotiate with people of a less liberal and more suspicious nature. Part of another regiment was hourly expected, to the commanding officer of which I should be necessitated to renew my application. Delay in every point of view being replete with danger, I hastened back to the wharf and candidly acquainted the master of the vessel with the foregoing circumstances, reminding him that, as a full authority still existed for his receiving me on board, he could not possibly incur any censure by the prosecution of our design as soon as the favorable moment offered to proceed on our destined course.

My arguments, though strongly urged, did not appear to produce conviction; he conceived a flag was absolutely requisite to protect him from being captured; and that by venturing to conduct me without that security he might entail ruin on himself and family. I attempted to combat his objections by alleging that the very circumstance of conveying a British subject who had undoubted credentials to secure the most favorable reception would effectually prevent any consequences prejudicial to his safety or his interest. I remonstrated to the wind; he appeared inflexibly determined; and it was with the utmost difficulty that at length I persuaded him to reflect maturely on the reasons I had advanced and to give me within two hours his ultimate resolution.

You will readily conceive the agitation of my mind during this painful interval, especially as a hint had been given me that the officer who commanded the galleys and who on repeated occasions had approved himself a zealous partisan had, in the course of the day, intimated an alteration of sentiment, relative to the measures necessary to be pursued, previous to my departure from the colony. This officer seemed to apprehend an application ought to be made on my part to the legislative authority; and that the permission which had been granted was insufficient without the sanction of the civil power. A journey to Williamsburg must have been the consequence of such an opinion being adopted; and, perhaps even then on representing my situation to the council of safety in that city it might have been thought expedient to apply to the government of Maryland for authentic documents to corroborate my assertions. Such a proceeding must inevitably have been attended with a tedious delay and with increased expense; not to mention the strong probability that a positive prohibition would have been the consequence of such a reference.

Under these peculiar circumstances it was absolutely necessary that I should appear perfectly collected in order to remove all suspicion of my pursuing indirect measures to accomplish my purpose. I therefore joined a party with whom I had occasionally associated since my residence in Hampton, and discussed with them the circumstance of the sudden departure of the battalion, and the objections unexpectedly started by the master of the vessel against receiving me without the formality of a flag. I acquainted them that an officer had accompanied me to the wharf, who had avowed his authority to be my conductor but was prevented from executing his commission by a sudden violent gale which had impressed his mind with apprehension of danger; therefore, conceiving the master fully justified in proceeding on the permission already granted, I requested the sentiments of those gentlemen with respect to the conduct necessary to be adopted for his entire satisfaction.

I was heard with the most obliging attention, and it appeared to be their unanimous opinion that I had complied with every requisite; that I was not actuated by any hostile intentions against America; that I had an undoubted right to avail myself of the most immediate opportunity to obtain a passage to Europe; and that the master of the schooner, who had been publicly engaged to convey me on board a British ship, could not possibly be subjected to any censure by the civil authority in Virginia; nor would he encounter any hazard with regard to the detention of his person and property by the officers and seamen in His Majesty's service.

Though I was happy in hearing sentiments so perfectly agreeable to my wishes, yet I experienced much agitation lest they might not prove effectual where it was immediately necessary they should be attended to; and a considerable time elapsed beyond the limited period before I received intimation that the party in question had made enquiry for me.

In an instant I determined to make this transaction a public concern and to receive his determination in presence of those who had so kindly evinced a solicitude for my welfare; he was therefore requested to enter the room and to deliver his opinion without reserve.

The undisguised conduct which I assumed on this very interesting occasion instantly operated in my favor. The master expressed his doubts in a less forcible manner, and they were answered by persons totally unconnected with my views, with whom he was well acquainted, and who could not possibly be governed by any motives prejudicial to his welfare or reputation. The event more than answered my expectations: the arguments adduced on my behalf, the persons by whom they were delivered, and the open manner in which I had submitted to investigation, carried conviction to his mind; he engaged to receive me without any further application and promised to be ready for me by the earliest dawn.

It was late before I retired to my apartment and then without the last propensity to partake of rest. I threw myself on the bed and yielded to a successive train of gloomy apprehensions. Indeed my situation was extremely intricate: early in the evening I had seen two persons whom I knew to be residents in Annapolis; I had endeavored to avoid them, but perceiving myself discovered I assumed an air of confidence, accosted them with apparent composure, and enquired after the welfare of several with whom I had been happily connected in better times. They knew I had taken my departure for the West Indies and appeared inquisitive concerning the motives which had occasioned my continuance on the continent. In brief terms I intimated the disappointment we had encountered, and the necessity of awaiting a more favorable opportunity; that the vessel was still lying in York River, and that I had been led into that neighborhood on a visit of friendship and curiosity.

Though my detail appeared to gain credit, I had some reason to conceive that they entertained suspicions of my real design, which they might consequently attempt to frustrate by immediate measures to my disadvantage. However I had sufficient resolution to invite them to my quarters, and obtained a ready assurance that they would see me early on the ensuing day to receive my commands for Maryland.

This event was an additional motive to urge dispatch; and it also pointed out the method necessary to pursue if I found the master of the vessel inflexible to my arguments: I determined in that case to receive my unwelcome visitors with an appearance of satisfaction, and if they were returning to Annapolis by way of Yorktown, even offer to accompany them to that place, as to the proper situation where I was awaiting an opportunity to proceed for the ocean.

Having, after our separation, succeeded in my plan of engaging an immediate conveyance to the nearest British ship, I well knew that the attempt without success would expose me to dangers and difficulties of the most alarming nature. My new-found acquaintance might be more early in their enquiries than was consistent with the plan I had adopted. On learning that I had amused them with a fallacious account an alarm might be instantly given which might occasion a pursuit; and a contrary wind or bad sailing might throw me into the power of those who would put the most unfavorable construction on my conduct; and perhaps punish me with a rigor by no means proportioned to the nature of the supposed offense. These painful ideas occupied my mind till the appearance of day. I was to receive notice when the proper period arrived for embarkation, and I waited the summons with equal impatience and anxiety. My baggage, which was contained in a small portmanteau, had been on board the vessel from the time I had engaged her for my passage; and two or three trifling articles which I had retained on shore were the whole of my encumbrance. About half past four a lad arrived with intelligence that all was ready for my reception. I delivered my parcel to his care and accompanied him to the adjacent beach, under no small agitation of mind, which it was highly incumbent on me to conceal by a steady appearance of confidence and serenity.

For the present I lay down my pen, but shall resume it by every convenient opportunity. Situated as I now am, I have full time to be circumstantial in my detail; an indifferent person might accuse me of prolixity, but I am persuaded you experience a real concern in whatever relates to my interest or happiness. Farewell!

LETTER XXXVI

On board the Emerald, *July 3, 1777*

The schooner destined for my conveyance was navigated by
an elderly man and by a youth about fourteen years of age.
With a view to guard against accidents, and to animate my
companions to perseverance, I had laid in a supply of refreshments for a voyage much longer than ours promised to
be, and we quitted the harbor with a favorable breeze and
the most pleasing prospect of an expeditious passage.

We had not proceeded far on our course before our attention was divided by the sight of two British frigates. One was
stationed in the vicinity of the capes, and the other at some
distance up the bay, in a situation to observe the movements
in York River. The former vessel being nearer to the sea appeared most eligible for my design, and to that we directed
our course accordingly; but scarce had we digested our plan
when the wind suddenly subsided and a total calm succeeded,
during the continuance of which we were unable to make
the least progress; about noon a strong breeze set in directly
opposite to our wishes; we made many tacks without seeming to obtain the least advantage; and though under this disappointment I suffered extreme agitation, yet had I resolution
to affect a perfect serenity that I might not increase suspicions
in the mind of my conductor, who could not avoid occasionally intimating his apprehensions that he encountered a
considerable hazard in the undertaking.

It is impossible to paint the distress that took possession of
my soul when the impracticability of reaching the ship, at

least that evening, was announced in the most decided terms. A strong head sea operated equally with the wind to baffle our best attempts; the master therefore proposed to return into the harbor and patiently await the event of the succeeding day. To this measure I strongly objected and recommended altering our course for the other vessel, which I conceived we could easily attain before the approach of night, but was exceedingly mortified to hear him explicitly dissent from my opinion, when no choice was left me but to return to an anchor in order to take the advantage of a more favorable opportunity.

This determination, so cruelly adverse to my hopes, rendered me almost frantic with apprehension. I recollected my Annapolitan acquaintance and the probability that they had excited an alarm on account of the deception I had practiced, from unavoidable necessity. I had also reason to entertain ideas of dangers and difficulties from every other quarter, and I knew not how to stem the torrent of adversity which appeared ready to overwhelm me. We were now before the wind, standing directly for the harbor, to which we were advancing with a very rapid progress; one expedient only remained, which a sudden thought suggested; I had plied my old pilot as freely with the bottle as was not inconsistent with our safety, and he evidently discovered, in consequence of it, a greater pliability of disposition. I availed myself of the important crisis, and under the plausible pretext of saving time, and being more ready to catch the first breath of a propitious breeze, I proposed running under a cliff to leeward of the town, where the riding was perfectly convenient, and where I trusted we might remain undiscovered till we could again, with propriety, resume our arduous undertaking.

To my infinite satisfaction, and indeed equal surprise, my plan received his immediate, and entire approbation; we were quickly at an anchor behind a point of land which entirely sheltered us from the view of the adjacent harbor; our little vessel was soon properly secured; the day closed with perfect serenity; and the veteran seaman and his boy, after partaking of such cheer as our stock afforded, calmly resigned themselves to repose without an anxious idea respecting the operations of the ensuing day.

Contrasted with mine, their situation was indeed most enviable; agitated by conflicting passions! by a continued series of disappointments, I tamely yielded to the pressure of calamity! and even dreaded the return of day, which was to expose me to new trials and probably to additional mortifications. I weakly anticipated a train of impending evils which I considered as unavoidable.

The night was uncommonly splendid. The beams of the rising moon were beautifully reflected on the noble expanse of water. Nature appeared perfectly serene; and every surrounding object contributed to elevate the imagination above terrestrial objects, to infuse a calm indifference with regard to sublunary events, and to suggest a firm confidence in the great, beneficent Creator! Yet harassed by the corroding reflections which incessantly intruded, I became insensible to all that could dignify the mind; the delightful prospect became a dreary waste; and I no longer recollected the providential deliverances I had so frequently and so unexpectedly experienced.

I attempted, but in vain, to compose myself and to obtain that rest so essential to recruit my agitated spirits for the transactions of the approaching morning; but every effort was ineffectual; I therefore determined to occupy the tedious interval by an excursion on the adjacent shore. Our vessel lay almost close to the beach, and a small canoe, which was fastened to our stern, enabled me in an instant to gratify my inclination. My comrades, exempt from every anxiety, were in perfect enjoyment of the most sound repose; and I landed without their being sensible of the intention I had formed. By this time the moon had nearly attained her meridian height; the hemisphere was decorated with unnumbered stars, and not an intervening cloud appeared to obstruct the view. I had attained a considerable eminence at no remote distance from the place of our anchorage; and from that situation I could plainly distinguish the town of Hampton; several vessels lying at the mouth of the harbor; an unlimited prospect of the Chesapeake; and, just rising above the horizon the British frigate, the object of my most ardent hopes! Such a grand assemblage of interesting objects gradually dissipated the gloom which hung over me; a returning ray of confidence took full possession of my soul; the eventful circumstances of my preceding days passed rapidly in review before my imagination; I yielded to an instantaneous impulse. I found myself unable to resist, and prostrate on the shore acknowledged the imbecility of human nature and implored the all-merciful Providence to support me under every future vicissitude and direct my wandering steps to the paths of peace and safety.

Supported and elevated by hope, I descended like a new being to the adjacent beach, and hastened along the shore to prepare for the ensuing enterprise. Scarce had I reached the vessel before the welcome dawn and a rising favorable breeze intimated the expediency of commencing our operations. I awakened my companions and apprised them of the promising gale: in an instant we were under way and stood with a pleasing prospect of success for the frigate, which during the preceding day had been the earnest object of our attention.

I now began to conceive that fortune, weary of persecuting me, was determined to make ample compensation for the mortification and disquietude I had sustained; but I was destined to encounter yet further trials under circumstances of more imminent danger.

When we were within two leagues of the ship, and at the moment that I was anticipating the happiness which

awaited me, the breeze suddenly headed us and quickly freshened to a perfect gale. Our schooner unfortunately was foul;
her sails and rigging in bad condition; and we had, in the
course of our former attempt, fully experienced her inability
to work to windward. In this dilemma a consultation took
place, the result of which was a determination to change our
course for the ship which was stationed up the bay; and the
master gave me great hopes that we should carry our point
without much difficulty if the wind continued steady in its
present quarter. To animate his exertions and attach him
more strongly to my interest, I promised a handsome aug-
mention to our stipulated agreement; and in return he assured me that he would persevere to the utmost, and at all
events not shelter in any harbor unless absolute necessity enforced him.

We had still serious embarrassments to encounter. A heavy
cross sea greatly impeded our progress and frequently broke
over the deck in an alarming manner. The wind also became
scant, and we barely lay our course. Hope, however, was predominant; I found we gradually gained on our object; my
comrades appeared confident of success; and I had a firm
persuasion that our expectations would be effectually gratified. Thus circumstanced, I resolved if possible to obtain a
short repose; the agitation of my mind and the extreme fatigue I had experienced had totally exhausted nature; I therefore summoned resolution to retire to my berth, having
previously given directions to be awakened before our arrival
at the ship; or if any unforeseen event should take place
which might require my attention or assistance.

It was about ten in the forenoon when I threw myself on
my pillow, and in a few minutes every anxious idea was
obliterated by a profound sleep; but scarce an hour had
elapsed before I was alarmed by a summons upon deck, and
in a tone which instantly filled my mind with a dread of impending evil. I sprung instantly from my cot and in a mo-

ment was too perfectly convinced that I had the strongest reasons to apprehend the most disagreeable consequences. We plainly descried an armed schooner stretching from the land with an evident intention to intercept our passage to the ship, from which we were at that time about two miles distant; and as she gained rapidly upon us, I began to abandon that confidence which had so recently taken possession of my breast.

Notwithstanding the depression which almost overpowered my faculties, I assumed sufficient resolution to animate my companions, which I seconded by promises of greater efficacy than the force of the most eloquent persuasions; and the wind veering a point or two in our favor, to my inexpressible joy we were within hail of the ship, when the American vessel was also within random shot, where she lay to, in order to watch our motions and take her measures accordingly.

At this critical period it blew a fresh of wind accompanied with a heavy swell of the sea; notwithstanding which, we run alongside the frigate with tolerable dexterity; but in attempting to catch a rope, which was flung from the deck, the boy had nearly fallen overboard, and before another could be thrown for our assistance, we had, in spite of every effort, fallen to leeward with astonishing rapidity. On a suspicion that we had acted by design, an officer directed us immediately to bring to, in a manner so commanding that we apprehended a shot would be immediately fired to force compliance. Obedience was only left us; but under our circumstances, obedience was attended with infinite danger; our anchor, though sufficient in smooth water, was by no means adapted for the present occasion, nor was the cable in a condition to bear the violent motion and working of the vessel; in several places it was greatly defective, and in its best state was only intended for harbors and occasional mooring places along the shore; necessity enforced submission; the anchor was let go, and for some moments I indulged hope that a boat would be manned and sent from the ship to learn the motives which had brought us into that perilous situation; but in that hope so reasonably founded I had quickly the mortification to experience a disappointment, we being again hailed in an authoritative manner and directed to send on board immediately.

Situated as we were, it was in vain to attempt representing the particulars which gave me a right to expect assistance and protection; we were unfortunately unprovided with a speaking trumpet, and the wind setting directly against us, it was impossible for the voice alone, at the distance we were from each other, to convery an articulate sound. Our canoe was of the smallest dimensions and could not, even in the most serene weather, contain more than one person with any degree of safety; tempestuous as it then was, the most imminent danger awaited the attempt; to deliberate was at least encountering equal hazard: should the vessel drift, it might be thought intentional, and a shot might be attended with fatal effects. I therefore entreated the master to undertake alone, without a moment's delay, the arduous enterprise, while I continued with his servant to render him every assistance in my power.

Whose situation was most critical I am utterly unable to determine; scarcely had the canoe put off before we became sensible that our vessel dragged upon the anchor, which induced my young associate to express the strongest fears that our cable could not possibly long hold out; in which case the least evil which threatened me was a tedious and probably a rigid imprisonment, as the armed schooner continued lying-to, at no remote distance, and in a very short time we must have drifted so far to leeward that she would have taken us even within random shot of that vessel to which I fled for refuge.

Under circumstances so peculiarly distressing I anxiously

attended to the motions of the canoe. The veteran seaman acquitted himself with the utmost dexterity. Sometimes from the height of the sea he was totally lost to view, which excited a momentary sensation of the most painful nature; but when I saw him rise with a rising wave, hope in consequence exhilarated my spirits. Though the distance was not far, near an hour elapsed before I beheld him ascending the side of the ship, every minute of which time, in my peculiar situation, appeared insupportably tedious. Meanwhile our little bark continued to pitch with great violence, and I was under continual apprehensions that the strands of our weak cable must inevitably yield to such excessive motion. Guess then my transport, when I heard the welcome signal given for hoisting out a boat. My eyes were riveted on an object which promised a speedy and effectual relief. I saw her launch from the ship with all the wild enthusiasm of joy! and in a few minutes I had the inexpressible happiness to take an officer by the hand, who delivered a friendly message from his commander with an obliging invitation to partake of every accommodation his situation could afford.

Thus much shall suffice for the employment of the present day; but I shall quickly resume the pen that I may conclude a narrative which I am persuaded you will consider interesting and eventful.

LETTER XXXVII

Emerald, *July 5, 1777*

The officer who had it in charge to convey me on board His Majesty's ship acquainted me that she was named the *Thames,* and was commanded by Captain Tyringham Howe, who had so remarkably distinguished himself in the defense of the *Glasgow* when she engaged the American fleet under the direction of Commodore Hopkins.

Against a force so wonderfully superior he maintained an animated contest; and in spite of their utmost exertions effected a gallant retreat into the harbor at Rhode Island. For his steady and intrepid conduct he was rewarded by a promotion into his present ship, which, I trust, will be only a prelude to some more honorable distinction.

By Captain Howe I was received with a cordiality which exceeded my utmost expectations. I gave him a brief detail of the events which had so happily terminated in placing me under his generous protection; and I entreated that he would render every assistance to the master of the schooner, by whose zealous and determined efforts I had accomplished an escape which opened the prospect of a speedy restoration to the blessings of domestic society.

In consequence of my requisition immediate orders were given to secure his vessel beneath the stern of the frigate; and my old pilot, with his faithful adherent, was received on board with assurances of every accommodation until a favorable opportunity presented itself of prosecuting their intentions with entire safety.

In about an hour after my arrival I sat down with Captain Howe and several officers to a plain but plentiful dinner; I experienced sensations I had long been unaccustomed to — my mind was exhilarated with joy and gratitude — I acknowledged the intervention of an all-directing Providence — and I enjoyed a rapid succession of these delightful ideas which indicated a reverse of fortune and an ample compensation for past solicitudes.

On my name being occasionally mentioned, it caught the attention of the first lieutenant, who, to my great astonishment, discovered a knowledge of my former situation. He particularly enquired concerning the welfare of my dearest wife and son, and assured me, with uncommon warmth, that every gentleman belonging to that ship had, even previous to the hope of any personal acquaintance, conceived sentiments highly advantageous to my character and my principles. Perceiving every countenance bore convincing testimony to the truth of such pleasing assertions, I was lost in amazement; and could not penetrate into the mystery which had so strangely secured to me the approbation and esteem of persons to whom I conceived I was totally unknown. I therefore entreated an immediate explanation, that I might learn how to render my grateful acknowledgments, and to approve myself deserving such an unexpected prepossession in my behalf.

Mr. R——, the gentleman who had so kindly expressed himself in my favor, then acquainted me that

a few weeks since, the *Thames* had taken an American vessel bound to a French island, on board of which were a number of letters, which had been examined with a view to obtain information; that in performing this duty they had met with two under my signature which had impressed them so strongly in my behalf that it was resolved to retain them till an opportunity offered for their safe conveyance. Accordingly, on the arrival of the ship at New York, they had been entrusted to the care of a German officer, with particular injunctions to deliver them immediately on the completion of his voyage.*

Mr. R—— concluded by observing that, the instant my name was mentioned, he entertained sanguine hopes that I was the person in whose cause they had been so strongly interested; and on finding those hopes so agreeably confirmed, he was persuaded every gentleman on board that ship rejoiced in the unexpected opportunity of affording protection and assistance where attachment operated so forcibly with duty to command their best exertions.

Had I not instantly conceived sentiments of regard for this worthy man, I must have been insensible to every generous, every grateful impression. I beheld him with a mixture of reverence and love — and tears, heart-felt tears — proclaimed the genuine, the fervent acknowledgments of my soul.

On board the *Thames* I continued until the 27th, experiencing from Captain Howe and the gentlemen under his command the most obliging attention and hospitality. But that ship being stationed a considerable distance up the bay, I became anxious for a removal into the *Emerald,* which lay in the vicinity of the capes, whose commander consequently had it more in his power to forward the intentions of those whose circumstances rendered it expedient to visit the city of New York.

Accordingly on the above day, an officer in an armed vessel having arrived on some duty from the commodore, I determined to embrace the opportunity of his return that I might obtain a situation nearer to the object of my hopes.

It was with difficulty I obtained the consent of Captain Howe and his benevolent officers to this necessary measure.

---

* Mr. R—— enclosed the intercepted letters in a very elegant and expressive epistle from himself; and they were punctually delivered. The author is at this time happy in including Captain R—— amongst his best and most valuable friends.

They suggested the probability of being speedily relieved and the pleasure they should receive in conveying me to my desired haven. Though I felt the full force of such persuasions, yet I combated their friendly arguments with reasons so justly founded that my hospitable protectors yielded reluctantly to their force; and with their sincere prayers for the completion of all my pursuits I bade them farewell; and early on the following day was received on board the *Emerald* with great attention and politeness.

I have now brought you to my present situation, where I experience every proof of regard and humanity. Since the commencement of this contest, I have repeatedly heard it asserted that the commanders of His Majesty's ship consider protection rather as an act of necessity than inclination; and that those loyalists who had, with infinite hazard, effected an escape from the adverse party had been treated by them, on application for refuge, with a distance and haughtiness that aggravated their sufferings and almost alienated their sentiments of allegiance. I verily believe the assertion in every instance most unjustly founded, propagated by malice and by republican artifice. On board the *Emerald* are several gentlemen under similar circumstances with myself; all equally strangers to our benefactors, we are all equally treated as friends and brethren. Captain Caldwell, who is the commodore on the station, is continually gaining on our esteem by the affability of his manners; his officers appear no less anxious to promote our entire satisfaction; and we meet with every accommodation our situation can possibly obtain. But kindly and humanely treated as I am, happiness is not yet my portion; my thoughts are anxiously turned towards you and our dearest boy, and I consider every hour a tedious delay till I obtain information of your health and welfare. Your letters will probably determine my future conduct. I trust I shall soon rejoin you in England; or by a pleasing change in the political system be enabled once more to bid you welcome to the continent of America. May Heaven grant us a speedy re-union, and may we pass the residue of our days without again experiencing the insupportable anxiety of separation.

New York, July 19, 1777

I have only a few minutes to inform you that yesterday I was safely landed in this city and met with the most cordial reception from our invaluable friends.

I found but one letter from my dearest wife, dated on the 26th of April and 1st of May last. On obtaining intelligence of your welfare, my joy was inexpressible. More than sixteen tedious months had elapsed since the date of your last; many of your epistles have undoubtedly miscarried; mine to you, I trust, have been more fortunate. During the remainder of our separation, our correspondence will be certain. I am now free, unawed, unrestrained. I feel myself enlarged; and I will write, speak, and act as becomes a zealous adherent to the British constitution.

In my next I will give you the particulars of my expedition hither; of my present situation; and probably some idea of my future intentions; but as the ship which is to convey this is preparing to sail, I must postpone further information.

Opportunities of writing from this place very frequently offer: expect therefore to hear from me again speedily. My voluminous detail will be delivered to you by Mr. S——, a worthy young man and a refugee from Maryland. To him I refer you for an account of your friends in that province, which he quitted but a few days since. Adieu.

LETTER XXXVIII

My last contained a circumstantial detail from the day of my quitting Maryland to that of my reception on board the *Emerald* frigate. I shall now continue my narrative to the time of my arrival in this city.

On the tenth of July, at day break, several vessels were distinguished which had passed us by favor of the night, and were stretching to the eastward with a crowd of canvas. In an instant we weighed anchor and stood out to sea. The *Senegal* sloop of war and an armed brig that were stationed off Cape Charles joined us in the chase, and before noon we took three large sloops and two schooners laden with tobacco, flour, and various valuable commodities for the French islands.

The capture of these vessels was a fortunate event to me and to those who were under similar circumstances, it being determined to send the prizes immediately to New York under convoy of the *Senegal* commanded by Captain Molloy.

On Friday the eleventh, Captain Caldwell introduced two gentlemen, who had escaped from Virginia, and myself, to the commander of the *Senegal*, and recommended us strongly to his kind attention. On board this ship we experienced every proof of hospitality and regard during the passage to New York, where on the 18th we were safely landed.

On entering the Narrows, my mind was forcibly struck

with the splendid appearance of a numerous and formidable equipment. A grand fleet, attended with innumerable transports arranged in their several divisions, lay at anchor off Staten Island. The island itself was covered with troops ready for embarkation, and every appearance indicated an expedition of the most decisive consequence. I could not avoid contemplating with astonishment the power — the apparently irresistible power — of the parent state; and in consequence, equal astonishment took possession of my mind when I reflected how ineffectual to every salutary purpose the most determined efforts had hitherto been.

Mr. and Mrs. C[hamier][1] insist on my sojourning beneath their friendly roof until some plan is adopted for a permanent situation, and express their regret that unavoidable events have so long detained me from experiencing their humanity and affection.

Mr. Chamier is no longer commissary general, having resigned that lucrative office with the greatest credit to his abilities and reputation, and is now auditor general of accounts, a station of equal honor but inferior in point of emolument; it is, however, attended with much less fatigue.

This alteration, though desirable to him, is particularly unfavorable to me. His patronage as commissary general was very extensive, and his inclination corresponded with his power to render me essential service. He has just acquainted me that he had, with a view to my interest, deferred for some time the filling up a profitable appointment; but learning that I had taken my passage by way of the West Indies, he had given up all hopes of seeing me in New York; and had, therefore, previous to his resignation, disposed of the employment to a gentleman who will, in all

[1] Daniel Chamier (d. 1778), whom Eddis had known in Maryland before the troubles, had left Baltimore because of loyalist sympathies and had taken a post with the British army in New York.

probability, acquire thereby an ample provision, should the war be continued for any length of time.[2]

Thus it appears that disappointment is still to destroy our hopes of prosperity. But it is folly — nay, it is criminal to indulge an idea of discontent. We have sufficient motives to nourish the most grateful acknowledgments; we will therefore look forward with increasing confidence, and trust to heaven alone for the disposal of every future concern.

It is impossible to conceive a more magnificent appearance than was exhibited by the departure of the grand fleet, which on the 23rd of last month weighed anchor and stood to the eastward with a favorable breeze. Whither they are bound is to the public an impenetrable secret; but if the consequences are what might be expected from the apparent strength of the armament, surely the day is at hand which will happily terminate the complicated miseries of this unnatural war.

There are those who appear sanguine enough to believe that the present campaign will assuredly prove decisive and restore the ancient government. It is certain that much may be expected from the operations of the formidable force under the command of Lord and General Howe; and the utmost anxiety and impatience prevail for intelligence of their destination and proceedings.

Our worthy friend has a delightful situation on the banks of the East River, about five miles distant from New York, where he principally resides during the summer. In this retirement I have a comfortable apartment where I enjoy rational society and an occasional retreat from the active scenes of military arrangements.

[2] Chamier had bestowed the post of commissary general on James Christie, refugee Baltimore merchant and friend of Eddis.

Wednesday, August 6

I have this instant heard of a vessel preparing to sail for Liverpool; I must therefore postpone an account of New York and its environs to a future opportunity. Every sail that I behold will excite the strongest emotions of expectation. Surely I shall now receive frequent accounts of your health and welfare.

York Island, August 16, 1777

Happy beneath this hospitable roof, I seldom visit the crowded city. At this season, the heat of the weather in town occasioned by the confined air and the reflection of the sun is scarcely supportable.

We are situated opposite to a fertile and beautiful part of Long Island. Vessels of every denomination are continually in view, and a variety of pleasing and interesting objects contribute to decorate the scene and to render our retirement truly delectable.

In the vicinity of our habitation is a very dangerous and narrow passage of the river, the sight of which excites ideas of greater terror than the celebrated poetical descriptions of Scylla and Charybdis. The tide runs with astonishing rapidity and in various currents, only one of which will carry a vessel through with any degree of safety; for on one side there is a shoal of rocks that barely make their appearance above the water; and on the other a dreadful vortex, occasioned by a rock several feet beneath the surface, which attracts and engulfs every object that approaches it. At particular periods of the tide this tremendous whirlpool appears to boil like foaming cauldrons, accompanied with a hollow terrific sound which impresses the most determined mind with apprehensions of inevitable destruction. The breadth of the river at this place is nearly half a mile, but that of the channel does not exceed eighty yards. This passage is only practicable at and near the height of tide; at any other time it would be extreme rashness to attempt it; and under the most favorable circumstances, the greatest knowledge and dexterity are requisite in the navigation.

Attended by some skillful boatmen, I had the curiosity to shoot this formidable gulf, which has, with some degree of propriety, obtained the appellation of *Hell Gate*. The velocity of our motion was indeed beyond credibility, through a wonderfully agitated stream accompanied with such dreadful roarings that, confident as I was in the skill of my conductors, I heartily repented the temerity of the undertaking, and beheld in imagination the invisible boundary "from which no traveller returns."

York Island [1] extends to Kingsbridge, about fourteen miles distant from the city, where it is joined to the continent by a small wooden bridge. The narrow deep river which runs at this place is a sufficient security against sudden incursions; and the works that are thrown up are so exceedingly strong, and in such commanding situations, as effectually to exclude the idea of a regular attack.

The capital of this province is situated on the southern extremity of the island: on one side runs the North and on the other the East River, on the latter of which, on account of the harbor, the city is principally built. In several streets trees are regularly planted which afford a grateful shelter during the intense heat of the summer. The buildings are generally of brick and many are erected in a style of elegance. The situation is said to be perfectly healthful, but fresh water is so very scarce that the purchase of this essential article is attended with a considerable expense.

Notwithstanding the war, New York is plentifully supplied from Long Island with provisions of all kinds. It must, however, be confessed that almost every article bears an exorbitant price when compared with that of former happy times. Both the North and East Rivers abound with a great

[1] By York Island he means Manhattan.

variety of excellent fish. Lobsters of a prodigious size were, till of late, caught in vast numbers, but it is a fact, surprising as it may appear, that since the late incessant cannonading they have entirely forsaken the coast, not one having been taken or seen since the commencement of hostilities.

Into this place and neighborhood, lobsters were introduced by accident; the province having been formerly supplied with them by the fishermen of New England, who brought them in well boats, one of which, in passing Hell Gate, striking against a rock, separated, and the lobsters, which escaped into their proper element, multiplied so exceedingly that in a short time the markets were amply and reasonably supplied.

Previous to the commencement of this unhappy war, New York was a flourishing, populous, and beautiful town. But immediately on the British troops taking possession, it was set on fire by some desperate incendiaries, and near a third part destroyed, in spite of the utmost exertions to prevent the spreading conflagration. The flames at the same instant burst out in a variety of places, which rendered it evident that this execrable deed was perpetrated from a principle of ill-directed zeal in order to preclude the royal army from a possibility of maintaining, with the least degree of comfort, their important acquisitions.

Notwithstanding the late devastation, there are still many elegant edifices remaining which would reflect credit on any metropolis in Europe. The new church is a noble structure; the college is spacious and convenient; the barracks are well built and well accommodated. The Dutch churches, with several places of worship for Protestants of different persuasions, reflect great credit on the genius of their architects; and the general style which predominates in this city impresses the mind with an idea of neatness and taste.

The numerous fortifications thrown up by the American troops in the vicinity of the capital appear to be constructed with judgment and attention. Why they were so precipitately abandoned is difficult to ascertain; indeed the whole island forms a continued chain of batteries and entrenchments which seemed to indicate the most resolute opposition.

I have lately made an excursion to Long Island and was highly entertained in my progress through a rich, beautiful, and well cultivated country. At a village named Flatbush, I met with several provincial officers belonging to the Maryland battalions, who had been taken in different actions and were prisoners on parole; and it was with real satisfaction I recognized some of my old acquaintance, and answered their respective interrogatories relative to their friends and connections in that province.

I have, in the course of my excursions, traversed the whole of York Island, and have even attended the relief of the piquet guard without Kingsbridge, which is the advanced post of the British army. It is impossible to convey an adequate idea of the interesting and noble objects which in every direction strike the curious and inquisitive eye. From the city of New York to the extent of the island, we beheld a regular continuation of formidable entrenchments. The troops appear animated in the service; and, surely, if their operations are properly conducted, the event cannot but effectually reestablish our ancient happy constitution on a permanent foundation.

I frequently partake of a military dinner, and have been hospitably entertained by the officers of different corps. As I have no real employment to occupy my time, I often change the scene. Variety of objects tends to prevent the intrusion of painful reflections; yet in spite of my best efforts, I am almost unable to stem the tide of sorrow when past blessings rise up like phantoms to my view and irresistibly remind me "that such things were, and that I once was happy."

I have written by Mr. S—— to Sir Robert Eden, and

have transmitted him a minute detail of the political state of Maryland.[2] I have represented leading characters with truth and impartiality; and have endeavored to convey a competent idea of the military arrangements and legislative dispositions which have taken place in consequence of the new system of government. He will probably give you his sentiments on the subject of my communications. This I can safely aver, that I have delineated circumstances in their true light, "nor set down aught in malice."

September 4

I am somewhat relieved from the anxiety I have experienced. Several letters mention the departure of a fleet for this port, under convoy of the *Bristol,* which left England previous to the sailing of the packet; consequently they may be hourly expected; by that opportunity I shall assuredly receive intimation of your health and welfare.

We have certain advice that our formidable armament has proceeded up the Chesapeake, and that the troops are landed in high spirits near the head of Elk. My friend Captain Howe, who has been here some time, expects sailing orders every minute and solicits me to accompany him on the cruise. Should he be directed to Maryland I have resolved to attend him; for if we obtain possession of that province, my duty and my interest will undoubtedly require my immediate presence. But to say truth, I cannot possibly adopt any plan with the least satisfaction until I procure information how it is with you and our dearest boy.

September 6

It is confidently reported that the city of Annapolis, the scene of our former happiness and prosperity, is by the inevi-

---

[2] This letter is reprinted in the *Maryland Historical Magazine,* 2, pp. 105-110.

table calamity of war reduced to ashes.[3] I need not observe that very many whom we have cause to love and esteem will most materially suffer in consequence of this unfortunate event. I am extremely anxious to learn the fate of our loyal friends who were necessitated by circumstances to remain in that place and in the neighborhood. I think it probable that on the appearance of the British fleet the adherents to government were compelled to retire to the interior country.

Captain Howe has not yet learned his destination, but should he proceed to the Chesapeake, it is my fixed intention to accompany him; by which means I shall obtain the knowledge of many material circumstances which it may be necessary to impart to our suffering brethren in England.

The provincials have lately made an attack on Staten Island, where during the first confusion they burned some stores and took a few prisoners; but they have paid severely for the attempt. The alarm instantly reached an adjacent post, and before they could effect a retreat they were vigorously attacked. About two hundred fell in the action, and near three hundred surrendered to the British detachment. Another party landed about the same time on Long Island, but on the appearance of opposition quitted it with precipitation. A strong body likewise advanced within sight of our lines at Kingsbridge, but retired on the approach of our light infantry. From these movements there is reason to believe that an attack was meditated on New York, in the absence of our grand army; but happily, a sufficient force is left to baffle the best concerted attempt.

September 13

I have impatiently expected particulars relative to Annapolis; but, as nothing further is yet circulated, I am inclined to

[3] This report was, of course, false.

indulge hope that the account which was propagated is without foundation.

Nothing of real importance has yet transpired from Lord Howe and the general, which is rather extraordinary, as we have had certain information of our troops having effected a landing at the head of the Chesapeake, and that they were in the vicinity of the American army.

A report is circulated that General Burgoyne has totally defeated the northern army under the command of General Gates.[4] If true, the consequences must be glorious and decisive.

The *Bristol* and her convoy are hourly expected, but by no one with more impatience than by your faithful, etc.

[4] Lieutenant General John Burgoyne (1722-1792) commanded what was essentially a task force based on Canada to effect a union with British forces in New York. Major General Horatio Gates (c. 1728/29-1806), recently appointed commander of the army opposing Burgoyne, blocked the route. The report Eddis had was not true; within five weeks Burgoyne had surrendered to Gates.

LETTER XL

We have intelligence of the most interesting and pleasing nature. It is said that General Washington has suffered a total defeat in the neighborhood of Philadelphia. Should this report, which is generally credited, be well founded, this destructive war will surely be quickly terminated.

I am happy to inform you that the account respecting Annapolis was totally without foundation. Hitherto Maryland has not experienced the actual scourge of war; may the sweet return of peace exempt her from participating in the almost general calamity.

On the appearance of the British fleet in the Chesapeake, the loyalists throughout that province were obliged to retire to a remote distance from navigable waters. There is certainly reason to credit this report, as I have only heard of two gentlemen who have eluded the vigilance of the ruling powers, and joined the royal army in their passage up the bay.

The *Thames* is sailed for the Chesapeake. I have been dissuaded from accompanying Captain Howe and my friends on board that ship by the earnest advice of Mr. Chamier, who justly observed "that as our troops had not made any descent on the western shore of Maryland, I could not render any essential service to myself or others by an excursion thither." But another reason more forcibly operates to detain me in my present situation — the constant anxiety I experience to obtain intelligence relative to the welfare of my dearest wife and son.

October 8

On Saturday last arrived the packet. Your letters, which informed me that you were well and happy, relieved my mind from a most painful and tedious state of disquietude.

On the same day an expedition took place under the command of Sir Henry Clinton[1] and Commodore Hotham. Their destination was up the North River, and this instant we have received the particulars of their operations. Fort Montgomery and Fort Clinton have been taken by storm; and in the capture of these places it was doubtful whether bravery or humanity was most predominant.

Count Gabrouski,[2] a young Polish nobleman who arrived in the late fleet from England, served as a volunteer in this expedition; and in those ranks where every individual displayed the utmost heroism, his distinguished coolness and intrepidity attracted universal admiration. In rushing forward to the enemy's works against a heavy and well directed fire, he received many wounds and fell at the foot of their entrenchments. His death was not immediate; he lived to rejoice in victory! The undaunted deportment of the British grenadiers excited his applause, even in the moment of dissolution. He spoke with rapture of that enthusiastic ardor which animated the whole as one body; and he desired that his remains might be deposited on the memorable spot

---

[1] Sir Henry Clinton (c. 1738-1795), second in command to Howe and after 1778 commander-in-chief of the British forces operating in the colonies.

[2] Eddis misplaced the "r" in the count's name, which is given in dispatches as Grabowski and Grabouskie.

where his gallant associates had gained such honor. It is said he entreated Lord Rawdon, in a very handsome compliment, to wear that sword which he had so recently drawn in support of the claims of Britain; and then paid the inevitable debt with that intrepidity of spirit which determined his conduct and led him forward to his fate.

It is expected the success which has attended this expedition will greatly facilitate the operations of General Burgoyne, who, after having surmounted infinite dangers and difficulties, has certainly advanced into the neighborhood of Albany.[3] Such variety of contradictory reports are daily circulated relative to the real situation of the army under his command that at present all is mere conjecture, without any certain ground on which to erect hope or admit despondency. There are those who conceive that General Howe ought to have conducted his first efforts to complete a junction with the northern army, and then to have directed the united force of the British arms wherever their exertions would have been most effectual. But without due information of those important facts that influence the proceedings of our commanders, it is illiberal and ungenerous to censure or condemn. The best concerted plans are frequently defective in execution; and the seeming hand of chance often leads to success the most brilliant and decisive.

November 1

At length *suspense* is determined by *certainty*. I am preparing for my immediate — perhaps final — departure from America. The unfavorable aspect of public affairs compels me to this necessary measure; and I must, in consequence, encounter the inconveniences of a winter's passage.

[3] Again Eddis was the victim of the rumor mill. Clinton's sortie did not help Burgoyne who was by this time bogged down at Saratoga.

But the predominant idea of being speedily restored to the society of a beloved wife and son will smooth the rugged billows and dissipate every apprehension of difficulty or danger.

General Burgoyne has been necessitated to surrender himself with his army. The particulars of this unhappy, unexpected event are not yet public; but it is strongly asserted that the want of provisions and not the amazing superiority of the enemy obliged our gallant general to submit to the inevitable fate of war.

An universal dejection has followed; every loyal countenance bears the most evident impressions of sorrow and disappointment. The exaltation of our adversaries is doubtless in full proportion to our mortification, for certainly this important success will animate their efforts in the prosecution of the war, give credit and strength to their political negotiations, and render dubious the event of a contest, which appeared rapidly approaching to a desirable issue.

The duty which fell to the share of General Burgoyne was infinitely more hazardous than the allotment of our other commanders; and, I am sorry to observe, it is the prevailing opinion that there has been some neglect in the proper arrangements necessary to have secured success. But leaving these matters, which are too high for me and enter not within my limited sphere of action, I shall confine my observations to domestic concernments.

A fleet is expected to sail from this place for Cork in about fourteen days, in which I have taken my passage on board a convenient vessel. An officer, and his lady, with whom I am intimately acquainted, bear me company in the voyage, so that before the conclusion of the year I trust we shall be reunited. May we never again experience the anxiety and sorrow of separation.

My worthy friend, under whose hospitable roof I have experienced every engaging mark of disinterested attachment, is determined if possible to increase my sense of the obligations I am under to him. Though comparative plenty abounds in this garrison, yet almost every needful article bears so exorbitant a price that in the present reduced state of my finances my proportion of stores for the passage to Europe would require a greater expenditure than I am well able to support. Mr. Chamier has therefore generously insisted on supplying me with every requisite; so that unless our voyage should be uncommonly tedious, I shall be enabled by his bounty to fare sumptuously every day. Perhaps within the extensive circuit of the British dominions there is not a character more universally beloved, or respected, than the exalted man to whom I am so deeply indebted.*

* This worthy personage was suddenly translated to a better state on the 27th of November, 1778. At that awful moment he was surrounded by some valued friends, and the instant before his dissolution he appeared in the full possession of health and cheerfulness. The author, on receiving intelligence of this fatal event, addressed the following letter to the Editor of the *Morning Chronicle,* which was inserted in that paper February 11, 1779.

Sir,

Through the channel of your extensive and impartial paper, permit me to offer a just tribute to the memory of an invaluable man, whose death will long be pathetically lamented and whose innumerable virtues endeared him, even in the midst of hostile commotions, to the love and veneration of contending parties.

Daniel Chamier, Esq., late auditor general to the British army in America, resided many years in the province of Maryland, and in the discharge of various important offices was particularly distinguished as a faithful servant to the public, and a valuable member of society.

On his quitting that government, to act in an honorable department in the service of the Crown, even the leaders in the present controversy spoke of him in terms of the highest veneration: they were assured that the uncommon benevolence of his disposition would extend to every person, independent of political tenets, who might be reduced by the vicissitudes of war, to implore his generous assistance.

When hostilities unhappily commenced between the parent state and her misguided colonies, this great! this worthy man! then exerted himself in a more exalted sphere! The loyalist who abandoned his family and property, compelled by the rigid hand of persecution, and who preferred his integrity to every inducement of avarice or ambition, found in him a sym-

It is advisable to guard against every possible accident. Our ship may be separated from the convoy and we may fall into the enemies hands; as in that case we shall probably be detained in some American port until an exchange takes place, I must entreat you to continue writing by every opportunity to New York, that at least a chance may be afforded me to hear of your welfare.

Should I have the happiness to arrive safe at Cork, I shall immediately send you intelligence, with an account of the course I intend to pursue in order to complete my voyage. But it is most probable I shall proceed directly to Bristol, which will be less expensive than by way of Dublin, and by which means I may be enabled to pay a melancholy visit to the monument of my once much beloved Powell! I shall also have the satisfaction to renew a personal connection with those valued friends who were solemn spectators of the

---

pathizing benefactor, by whom he was hospitably received, his necessities amply supplied, and every relief extended that his fortune or influence could possibly afford.

The prisoner experienced no less the effects of his unlimited compassion: amongst those who were captured by the incidents of war many were the husbands, the sons, and friends of them with whom he had been formerly connected. By his interest he procured them particular indulgences; he advanced considerable sums for their immediate occasions, and exerted every effort to alleviate the idea of captivity and render them comfortable in their peculiar situations. In a word, the utmost hospitality marked the whole of his conduct, and the innate goodness of his heart beamed forth in every action.

Such was the man for whom the prayers of multitudes were fervently offered; but, alas! the will of heaven suddenly removed him from this terrestrial state, to receive an eternal recompense for his faithful discharge of every relative duty.

To enter fully into the character of this very excellent person would greatly exceed my abilities and lead me into a field of prolixity. Suffice it to say that in him his sovereign has lost a most loyal animated subject; his country an invaluable citizen; his wife a tender indulgent husband; and the writer of this letter (with numbers who have felt the miseries of this unnatural contention) has lost the most faithful affectionate friend! the most generous humane benefactor!

concluding scene of that celebrated actor's life, which so strongly evinced the force of the ruling passion even under the awful circumstances of death.*

Adieu. Be constantly prepared for my reception, and believe me unalterably yours.

* See Letter II.

LETTER XLI

Cork, December 16, 1777

Thanks to Almighty God I am safely arrived at my desired
port, after a pleasant and expeditious passage.

On the 15th of November I took an affectionate leave of
our generous hospitable friends; on the 18th we quitted the
coast; on the 13th instant we struck soundings; and yesterday in the evening landed at a village named Passage,
took post horses, and were set down in this city in time to
procure a good supper and convenient lodging.

The hurry and bustle of this place bears some resemblance
to our great metropolis. The streets are crowded with busy
multitudes; many of the shops have a handsome appearance; and the habitations of the principal merchants sufficiently indicate their wealth and commercial importance.
The incredible quantities of provisions, which are preparing for exportation, cannot but excite the highest ideas of
the trade and consequence of this flourishing port. The variety of canals, bridges, and wharfs are likewise deserving
of admiration. By their canals, ships of considerable burden
are laden at the merchant's doors; and the wharfs, which
are convenient and extensive, are covered with innumerable
commodities, principally for the supply of the army and
navy in America.

By my friend Mr. Chamier I was favored with a letter of
introduction to Mr. B——, a merchant of great respectability in this port, from whom I have received a frank and gen-

eral invitation to his table during the time that inclination or necessity may detain me in this city.

There are few persons in whom the passion of curiosity is more predominant than in myself; and the environs of Cork promise abundant gratification to an inquisitive mind; but as the first object of my pursuit relates to you and to our dearest boy, I have no wish for an opportunity to make any excursion foreign to the thoughts that engross my mind in my present situation.

Passage, December 25

Yesterday I took leave of Cork, and came to this place in order to embark for Bristol. About noon we expect to sail.

I shall quit Ireland with deep impressions of gratitude. The entertainment I have experienced greatly exceeds the high ideas I had been taught to form of Irish hospitality. May they continue to enjoy every blessing which liberty, industry, and prosperity can afford.

I shall leave this to be forwarded by the post. Should a favorable gale crown my wishes, it is possible — nay, probable — that I may be happily reunited to my dearest partner before she will receive this fervent assurance of my unalterable attachment. The hour — the long expected hour — is at hand, which will restore to us the blessings of domestic felicity. Adieu.

LETTER XLII

Ilfracomb, Devon, December 27

I am safely landed on my native shore. The post departs for London within an hour; I gladly embrace the opportunity to give you an account of my safe arrival and explain the circumstances which occasioned an alteration in my intended route.

I embarked at Passage on Christmas-day, but the wind would not permit us to sail till the ensuing morning. From thence to the Isle of Lundy we had a prodigious run, having accomplished near fifty leagues in about twenty-four hours. The wind then became contrary and we were happy to gain this harbor, where the master of the vessel means to await an alteration of weather in his favor.

The distance from this place to Bristol is reckoned twenty-five leagues; but on account of the strong tides which prevail in this channel, short as the passage is it cannot well be attempted against an adverse wind; and as present appearances do not indicate a speedy change, I have determined to resign the plan of prosecuting the voyage, and shall therefore depart by land the instant my baggage has passed the necessary examination.

When you receive your husband to your faithful arms, let every anxious idea be excluded — let us unite in recounting past deliverances and be thus animated to look forward with gratitude and confidence. Our disappointments and our misfortunes have originated from inevitable causes; and if adversity should still continue to oppose our best endeavors, we must derive consolation from reflecting that we have acted consistent with the sentiments which we professed, and with a conscientious regard to the duties of that station in which Providence had placed us, always remembering that though

> 'Tis not in mortals to command success,
> They may do more —— DESERVE IT.

INDEX

INDEX

234

INDEX

THE JOHN HARVARD LIBRARY

*The intent of
Waldron Phoenix Belknap, Jr.,
as expressed in an early will, was for
Harvard College to use the income from a
permanent trust fund he set up, for "editing and
publishing rare, inaccessible, or hitherto unpublished
source material of interest in connection with the
history, literature, art (including minor and useful
art), commerce, customs, and manners or way of
life of the Colonial and Federal Periods of the United
States . . . In all cases the emphasis shall be on the
presentation of the basic material." A later testament
broadened this statement, but Mr. Belknap's interests remained constant until his death.*

*In linking the name of the first benefactor of
Harvard College with the purpose of this later,
generous-minded believer in American culture the
John Harvard Library seeks to emphasize the importance of Mr. Belknap's purpose. The John Harvard
Library of the Belknap Press of Harvard University
Press exists to make books and documents
about the American past more readily
available to scholars and the
general reader.*